Musical Scales of the World

Dr Michael Hewitt

THE NOTE TREE
thenotetree.co.uk

Dr Mike Hewitt

First printing: 2013

ISBN:0957547005
ISBN-13:9780957547001

DEDICATION

This book is dedicated to my son Ashley Hewitt.

CONTENTS

Section 4: Greek Folk Music: Dromoi...112

Section 5: Pentatonic Scales...125

Section 13: Scales of Carnatic Music...224

Section 14: Invent Your Own Scales...299

ACKNOWLEDGEMENTS

Thanks are due to all of the musicians and/or scholars who have directly or indirectly contributed to the content of this book. Special thanks are due to K. Krylov for his brilliant thesis on the use of harmony in Bulgarian music; the Tcherepnin Society for its information on the musical scales used in the musical language of Techerepnin; Michael Tenzer for his informative explanations of modern developments in Balinese musical scales; Wayne Vitale for his insightful observations on Balinese scales; Anthony King for his detailed accounts of the tuning of individual kora scales; Ezra Abate of the Jared Music School of Ethiopia for his clear explanations of Ethiopian pentatonics and Dr Vidyadhar Oke for his vast knowledge of Indian classical music scales.

Introduction and Preliminary Concepts

I have never met a musician or composer who is not fascinated by the subject of musical scales. This fascination probably begins when they discover that the major and minor scales, which were largely inherited from Western classical music, are but a few out of what are possibly hundreds of different scales which musicians are capable of using. These include the diatonic modes originally used by the Christian church prior to the rise of the major and minor system; a large group of so-called artificial, synthetic or exotic scales; the scales used in jazz and blues; pentatonic scales of different types used in many parts of the world and many, many others.

This book has been written to satisfy the curiosity of those musicians who wish to know more about such scales and where they come from. Although there are potentially thousands of such scales, this book will consider the main musical scales that modern Western musicians and composers have used or at least experimented with over the last century or so. This includes scales from different musical cultures which Western musicians have often been eager to try out themselves. In order to do this, these scales are often brought over into a Western format in order to make them more readily accessible and usable. In some cases, these scales require special types of tuning. The scales used by Indonesian Gamelan orchestras are a good example of this Where such types of tuning are indispensible to the use of the scale concerned, the exact method of tuning will be given.

Unfortunately, within the space of a single book it is impossible to consider every single musical scale that has ever been used. The scales of ancient Greek music for example, are not discussed here, as they are a rather specialized area of study. Neither are the maqamat of Middle Eastern music discussed at length. This is because, in similarity with the ragas of Indian classical music, maqamat are not musical scales as we

1

commonly understand them, but more properly a set of melodic frameworks for extemporization. frameworks that cannot be mastered overnight or without the guidance of a properly qualified teacher.

Even excluding these however, there is enough material in this book to keep the scale curious musician busy for a long period of time.

Preliminary Concepts

Before considering specific musical scales, it is advisable to study a number of preliminary concepts, as these can help the musician make the most effective and practical use of the scale concerned. The first of these is the importance of the interval of the **octave**. The octave is well known to most musicians as the interval between a given note and its re-appearance on a higher or lower level of the pitch register. We can appreciate this through reference to the following illustration:

Octave Interval

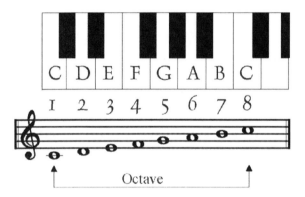

As can be seen, beginning with note C, it is possible to count up successive steps of the musical scale – D, E, F, G, A, B - until the eighth step is reached, where note C appears again. Consisting of eight steps, the interval between the two appearances of note C is therefore called an octave.

Once the octave is reached the scale pattern simply repeats itself upon a higher or lower level of the pitch register. Because of this, a given musical scale only needs to be defined within the space of one particular octave. Indeed, although there are instances of scales patterns which exceed the range of the octave, these are few and far between. Most musical scales in the world span an octave, after which the pattern of the scale repeats itself in subsequent octaves.

Here therefore it is useful to conceive the octave as being but a single turn of a spiral. The spiral as a whole represents the pitch register which begins with the lowest audible notes used in music and ends with the highest. One turn of this spiral would therefore appear as a circle around the circumference of which the notes of the scale can then be placed. In the case of the major scale therefore, the scale would appear as shown in the following illustration:

Major Scale Expressed Within Octave Circle

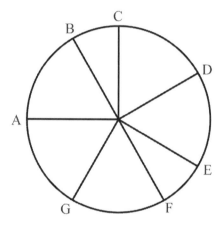

Between adjacent notes of the scale is a **scale step**. This step will be of a particular size, this size being expressible as a proportion of the octave space. In terms of the octave circle this translates into the size of the arcs. The larger arcs in the above diagram therefore designate scale steps of a tone, while the smaller arcs designate scale steps of a semitone.

The next concept to consider is the concept of **scale degree**. Generally a scale will be considered to begin with a particular note. This beginning is therefore designated as the first degree of the scale. Functionally, this first degree will generally be treated as the tonic note i.e. the central note of the scale. Being the central note, the first degree will therefore represent the most important degree of the scale.

In the case of the major scale just considered therefore, note C will be taken to be the first scale degree, note D, the second scale degree, and so on. The scale will therefore be complete after a return to the first degree in the next octave up:

Scale Degrees

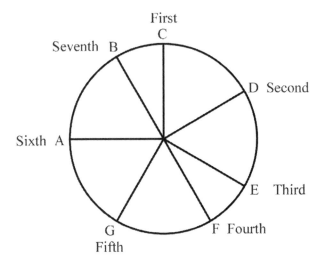

A pentatonic scale, which only has five notes, will therefore only have five scale degrees, while a hexatonic scale of six notes will have six, etc..

The essential difference between a scale and a mode is the next point to consider. Although musicians often use the terms scale and mode interchangeably, there is a subtle difference between the two. In order to avoid confusion, this difference is best explained and clarified at the outset.

A scale is a pattern of scale steps which divide the octave into a certain number of scale degrees. In the case of the major scale beginning with note C (shown in the preceding diagram) this pattern of scale steps is: tone, tone, semitone, tone, tone, tone and semitone. This can be easily seen by looking at the size of the arcs within the circle.

When speaking of a mode a particular note of the scale is implied as a tonic or ground note. Looking again at the previous diagram it is easy to see that feasibly, any one of the seven notes could be chosen to be the tonic. Once a tonic note has been selected, a particular mode of that original seven note scale is implied. This mode will have a different pattern of scale steps. If C is chosen to be the tonic, the pattern is tone, tone, semitone, tone, tone, tone, semitone. However if note A is chosen to be the tonic the pattern is tone, semitone, tone, tone, semitone, tone, tone. This essential difference is one not of scale, but of mode, the former pattern yielding the major mode, the latter pattern the natural minor mode.

Where scale is concerned therefore, the main point of interest is the pattern of scale steps of different sizes that define that scale. Where mode is concerned however, the main focus of interest is the relationship of each note to the tonic, a mode being a sum of these relationships.

Each mode will have a particular modal feeling, colour or atmosphere. In ancient Greek music this was referred to as the modal ethos. In terms of modern usage, the perceived ethos of a mode is largely a result of the relationship of the individual notes of the scale to the tonic note. Generally augmented and major intervals help to produce a bright modal color, while minor and diminished intervals produce a dark color. The major mode, in which the second, third, sixth and seventh are all major intervals, is therefore a brightly colored mode, while the natural minor mode, where the third, sixth and seventh are minor intervals, is therefore a darker colored mode.

When studying any mode therefore, it will greatly benefit the musician to carefully analyze the relationship of its particular notes to the central tonic note. This analysis is made by working out the individual intervals between each modal tone and the tonic.

Another important preliminary concept is the **tetrachord**. Not all cultures view musical scales as a ladder of eight notes rising up through the octave. A lot of very early music had a small range of only a few notes. As this range expanded, so musical scales began to be created.

However, one of the first stages on the way to the creation of fully-fledged musical scales was the tetrachord, a group of four notes spanning a fourth. In ancient Greek music this unit of the tetrachord was at one time the main focus of musical theorists and philosophers interest. A scale such as the major scale for example, would have been viewed as a sum of two tetrachords. As there was a whole tone separating them, these were called disjunct tetrachords:

Major Scale as Sum of Two Tetrachords

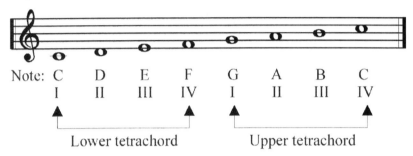

Most seven note scales can be analyzed in terms of their tetrachordal composition. This type of analysis is made by seeing how the fourth in each tetrachord is divided. In case of the major scale shown above the fourth of the lower tetrachord is divided into two tones and a semitone in this order: tone, tone, semitone. The upper tetrachord divides the fourth in the same way. The application of this will become evident later in this book where we will look more closely at the tetrachordal composition of particular scales.

The final concept to consider is **transposition**. With each of the scales/modes presented in this book will be given a transposition pattern. This pattern expresses the sizes of each of the scale steps in semitones. A tone will therefore be expressed by a 2, a semitone by a 1. Therefore the transposition pattern for a major scale is 2 – 2 – 1 – 2 – 2 - 2 – 1. Using this transposition pattern it is therefore possible to work out the major scale, or indeed, if the transposition pattern is known, any other scale, beginning on any key note that we choose.

Therefore say for example that we want to build a major scale on Eb. We can apply the transposition pattern as follows:

- 2 semitones up from Eb gives note F;
- 2 semitones up from note F gives note G;
- I semitone up from G gives note Ab;
- 2 semitones up from Ab gives note Bb;
- 2 semitones up from note Bb gives note C;
- 2 semitones up from C gives note D;
- I semitone up from note D gives note Eb.

In this way we have just generated a major scale in the key of Eb:

Scale of E Flat Major

Scales of any other type may be generated upon any keynote by simply applying the transposition pattern for that scale to the chosen keynote.

Having studied some of these preliminary concepts we will now proceed to a study of the main scales of world music, as currently used and recognized by Western musicians. Be aware however, that the learning curve of this study can rise very steeply. Therefore while efforts have been made to keep explanations as simple as possible, please bear in mind that some features of this subject cannot be grasped from a single reading of this book. Consequently, in some cases further study and research may be required on behalf of the reader. Playing the scale on an instrument will also help a great deal, while attempts to compose some music using a given scale would be even more helpful for the reader, for this will give the reader a direct experience of the particular modal colour produced by a given scale.

Section 1: Musical Scales of Western Classical Music

The most important scales that are, or have been used in Western music are probably the major, minor and chromatic scales. The foundations for these scales were clearly established by the classical music repertoire belonging to the Baroque, Classical and Romantic periods of Western music history, a period that lasted over 250 years. Although in modern classical music of the twentieth and twenty-first century, the major and minor scales in particular, have played a much lesser role, so far as Western popular and dance music is concerned, the major and minor scales are still used on a regular basis. For this reason, the major and minor scales provide an ideal place with which to begin the study of the musical scales of the world.

The Chromatic Scale

If I start by playing note C on the keyboard, and then I play every single key – both white and black – in immediate succession – when I arrive at the next note C an octave higher I would have played a complete chromatic scale. The chromatic scale therefore uses every single note on the keyboard. Ordinarily though, when writing a piece of music, a selection of notes will be made that does not necessarily include all twelve notes. In this way, the chromatic scale itself is of the order of a *foundation scale*. This means that the notes used by other scales – such as the major or minor for example - are selected from the notes available in the chromatic scale.

This makes the chromatic scale *the* most important scale used in Western music. Whatever style of Western music is being considered the notes for this music will in all probability be drawn from the chromatic scale. Bearing this in mind, let us now look at some of the features of the chromatic scale, beginning with the gap or interval between each of its notes.

The gap between adjacent steps of the twelve-tone scale is a uniform gap of a semitone. The chromatic scale thus results from the division of the space of the octave into a series of twelve equal semitones.

Virtually all of the music written since the establishment of the Western tonal system during the sixteenth and early seventeenth centuries uses the twelve-tone chromatic scale. Moreover, even today, anybody who writes or produces music in the Western world will probably be using the twelve-note chromatic scale. Consequently, all fretted or keyed Western musical instruments are manufactured with the assumption that the user will be, or will wish to be, using the twelve-toned chromatic scale for the purposes of writing, playing or producing their music.

In the case of plucked instruments such as the guitar, a series of fixed frets are placed along the fret board, which enables the guitarist to move up and down in semitones within the chromatic scale. This means there are twelve such frets for each octave of sound, making each fret equivalent to a key on a keyboard.

Because musical instrument manufacturers assume that the chromatic scale is going to be used, should the user wish to employ a different type of scale, or a different kind of division of the octave, they will then encounter certain problems. For example, a musician might wish to play an Arabian *maqam*. Some *maqam* use three-quarter tone intervals, which cannot be played on a piano or guitar limited to the twelve-tone chromatic scale. Should the musician wish to write or play music using such a *maqam* they will therefore have to employ a different instrument. They must either use instruments which are not fretted or keyed i.e. fretless guitars, strings or the human voice, or else use an instrument such as the oud, specifically built to play those subtle microtones used in Arabic modal music.

Here perhaps it is fortunate that many composers, songwriters and music producers tend to write their music within the bounds of the twelve-tone chromatic scale. Indeed, many do not question this, giving no thought whatsoever to the fact that there might be any alternative.

Now as far as the main body of Western music is concerned this assumption is mostly correct. However, there are many non-Western styles of music that use completely different scales and methods of tuning. Therefore, it is perhaps unwise to think that the twelve-tone chromatic scale has any sense of permanency, inevitability or universal status.

The Major Scale

Not all twelve notes of the chromatic scale are necessarily used within a particular composition. Usually a subset of those twelve is used. This subset is obtained by selecting from those twelve notes the notes required for the composition. In this sense, the chromatic scale can be viewed as a repository of available notes.

One of the most popular and enduring subsets of the chromatic scale of Western music is the *major scale*. The major scale is and has been used in virtually every single genre of Western music, ranging from classical, folk, rock, pop, dance music, etc. In fact, the major scale is probably one of the most important and enduring musical scales that has ever been used in Western music. In the main, this is due to its remarkable musical qualities.

The major scale divides the octave up into seven scale steps, represented by the seven letters of the musical alphabet starting with C. Of the seven notes of the scale, the first degree is generally considered the most important, signifying as it does the tonal centre of the music. Accordingly, within Western music the first degree of the scale is given the title *tonic* in indication of this fact.

The Importance of the Tonic

The use of a tonic note, especially as the first degree of a particular scale, occurs in many different types of world music. However, although the term 'tonic' might not always be used, the general function indicated by the word 'tonic' often is. For this reason, it is useful when studying musical scales, to gain a clear idea of what the tonic is and what it does.

At a general level, the word *tonic* refers to the tonal centre of a piece or passage of music. In other words, the tonic is a central point of reference that the ear uses to make sense of the melody. This it does by relating the notes of the melody to the central tonic note. When music is composed in such a way, it is said to have a tonal centre or sense of tonality. Even though we may not be consciously aware of this, everybody uses this sense of tonality when listening to music. This is how we recognize that the music is in a *key*. Although we may not be able name the key, we still recognize that there is a key due to our instinctive recognition of the presence of a tonic note.

Aesthetically speaking, a tonally driven melody is far more satisfying to us than a melody that simply wanders aimlessly from note to note. Having a sense of tonal drive, the melody can then more easily acquire a clear sense of direction and form. This in turn gives us the impression that the melody represents a journey endowed with a clear purpose.

In many ways, the tonic note is analogous to the number one in the numerical series. Without the number one, no other number is possible. Once one has been defined however, all other numbers acquire an automatic value thereby. This value is determined by their relationship to the number one. In this sense, the number one represents the very centre of the world of number, without which no other number could have any meaning or significance.

Endeavoring to explain the precise function of the tonic, the German twentieth century composer Paul Hindemith (1895 – 1963) likened the tonic note to the sun around which the planets of the solar system revolve, or alternatively the comparatively dense mass of the atomic nucleus around which spins all of the electrons[1]. Both of these are excellent analogies, as they place the tonic note at the very centre of the musical dialogue, a centre surrounded by its various satellites, which are the other notes of the scale.

---

[1] Paul Hindemith, *The Craft of Musical Composition*, Vol. 1.

Hindemith was not alone in making this comparison. The English composer and folklorist Cecil Sharp similarly described the function of the tonic as a dominating influence over the other six notes. Using the analogy of the solar system he regards the seven notes of the scale as consisting of six planets orbiting and owning allegiance to a central sun.[2]

When a piece of music is organized tonally in this way, it is said to have a *key* or a *keynote*. The keynote corresponds to the note that functions as the tonal centre. Therefore, music in the major scale, which uses note C as the tonal centre, is said to be in the *key* of C major.

A scale degree is a particular note of the scale. Having seven notes, the major scale therefore has seven degrees. These are customarily numbered from I to VII rising up from the tonic note. The tonic note is therefore the first degree, as shown in the diagram below:

Degrees of the Major Scale

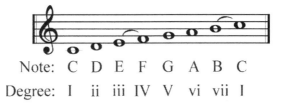

Note: C D E F G A B C
Degree: I ii iii IV V vi vii I

Notice that some of the scale degrees are represented in lower case numerals. These are the degrees of the scale which provide the root for a minor (or in the case of chord vii a diminished) chord, as opposed to those represented by numerals in upper case, which represent the roots of major chords. However, as this is an issue of harmony, rather than scale, no more that is strictly necessary will be said about this here.

---

[2] Cecil Sharp, *Some Characteristics of English Folk Song*, p. 136.

Between each scale degree, there is a scale *step*. Not all scale steps are the same size. Between the first and second degrees of the major scale, there is a gap of a whole tone – equivalent to two semitones. Between the second and third degrees, there is also a gap of a whole tone. Between the third and fourth scale degrees however, there is a gap of a semitone, which is half of the size of a whole tone. Subsequent steps are all whole tones, until we reach the seventh scale step, which is again a semitone. This information is portrayed diagrammatically below:

Tones and Semitones in the Major Scale

1	2	3	4	5	6	7	8
C	D	E	F	G	A	B	C

1   1   1/2   1   1   1   1/2

1 = Whole tone

1/2 = Semitone

As the scale is composed of two sizes of scale step, melodies that use this scale have a certain variety and fluidity of movement, which gives them great appeal for the ear. The semitones are those points in the scale where there tend to be definitive leanings towards the note above or below. The most important of these is the semitone gap between the seventh and eight steps, which gives the seventh degree of the scale a nice tendency to rise up towards the tonic note C. Accordingly the seventh note of the scale acts as an important supporter of the tonic function. For this reason, it is called the *leading note*, as it functions melodically as a leader up to the tonic. By so doing, the leading note thereby highlights the importance of the tonic as the keynote.

A composer may use the major scale in any key required. For this purpose, each note of the twelve-tone chromatic scale can be used as a tonic note in its own right. This means that there are at least twelve possible major keys, each key differing in terms of the note chosen as tonic. I say at least, because it is possible to write music in enharmonically equivalent keys i.e. the key of C sharp major and the key of D flat major. Because C sharp and D flat are enharmonically equivalent notes, in actuality both keys use the same keynote - although we do need to bear in mind that they would appear differently on a musical score.

When a composition uses say, note B flat as the tonic note the key is said to be B flat major, while if note D is taken to be the tonic, the key is said to be D major. Both of these keys are illustrated in the diagram below. Notice that both keys employ the same characteristic sequence of scale step sizes relative to the tonic note. In this way, the only difference between the different major keys is their relative pitch, this being determined by the position of the keynote in the scale.

Major Keys of B flat and D Major

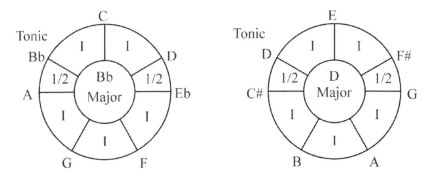

The Natural Minor Scale

Another example of a familiar subset of the twelve-note scale is the *minor scale*. Like the major scale, the minor scale has played a tremendously important role in Western music. The importance of this scale is due not just to its remarkable musical qualities, but also because it provides an important modal alternative to the major scale. Indeed, the major and the minor scales between them, define the modal totality of Western tonal music.

The minor scale also has seven notes, which can be notated using the same seven letters of the musical alphabet as the C major scale except that this time we start with A rather than C. As such, both C major and

A minor use the same set of notes. The difference between them is therefore simply a matter of placement of the tonic. The diagram below illustrates this essential difference between the major and the minor scales. At the top the major scale can be seen whose tonic note is C. Using the same range of notes we can then obtain the minor scale – shown at bottom – by transferring the tonic to note A.

A Natural Minor Scale in Comparison with C Major Scale

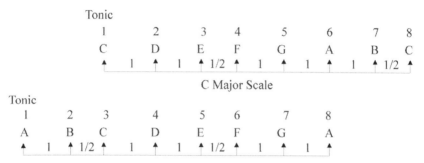

Because of the different position of the tonic note in A minor, this means that in the A natural minor scale there is a different order of scale step sizes. This gives to the A minor scale a contrasting sense of character and mood. Therefore, in a conventional sense we find that the major scale is particularly suited to the expression of bright and sunny feelings while the minor scale is more suited to the expression of darker and more somber feelings - although this is of course a simple generalization, which cannot be applied in all instances.

This audible difference of mood between the two scales occurs because of the different interval relationships occurring between the various degrees of the scale and the tonic note. This in its turn shows that on a second level, the tonic performs another important function. While on the first level, the tonic note serves to define the key, on the second level, the tonic note is the agent that enables the mode to be recognized. By mode is meant the difference say, between the major and minor scale. Both may use the same tonic note, yet they sound different, the major sounding brighter the minor darker. This is a difference of *mode*, the word mode being strongly related to the word mood. As this important, it will now be explained further.

At the first level, each degree of a scale may be regarded to be simply a note. As a note, the pitch of each scale degree can be defined – say for example note G. On the second level, each note of the scale signifies a particular interval relation with the tonic. Therefore, in the key of C, note G signifies the interval relation of a perfect fifth. This is far more that being just a note. Bearing this relationship to note C, note G then acquires an expressive value within the scale as a whole. The sum of such values with respect to a given scale defines the mode of that scale – in this instance whether major or minor.

Therefore, in the major scale, the third, sixth and seventh degrees of the scale form major intervals with the tonic note. This gives to those notes a characteristic brightness of expression that contributes greatly to the distinct modal qualities of the major scale. Similarly, in the minor scale the third, sixth and seventh degrees are all minor intervals. This gives to those notes a darker, more somber character of expression, which is all a part and parcel of the minor mode.

These differences in interval relation between the major and minor modes account for the differences of mood associated with each scale. Like the major scale, the minor scale can be used in any required key. This means that the twelve-tone chromatic scale offers an array of twelve possible keynotes for the minor key. A piece that uses the minor scale upon the keynote of G is said to be in the key of G minor, while one which uses the same minor scale, but on the keynote of B is said to be in the key of B minor.

Having considered some of the more general features of the major, minor and chromatic scales, let us now consider each of these scale on an individual basis, beginning with the major scale.

The Major Scale

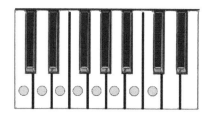

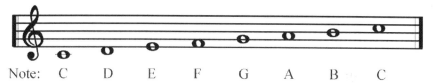

Note: C   D   E   F   G   A   B   C

Origin: European.

Scale Type: Heptatonic diatonic.

Tuning: Equally tempered.

Styles of Music: All Western styles.

Transposition: 2 – 2 – 1 – 2 – 2 – 2 - 1.

Features: The major scale is probably one of the most popular and enduring scales of Western music, a scale that is now used in virtually every single style or genre of music. The scale illustrated, as all subsequent scales in this book, is in the key of C, which means to say note C is the first degree of the scale – the tonic note.

The major scale is distinguished from every other type of scale because of the pattern of intervals formed by each note of the scale and the tonic note. In the case of C major depicted above, these are note D – forming a *major second* with the tonic, note E – a *major third*, note F – a *perfect fourth*; note G – a *perfect fifth*; note A – a *major sixth* and finally note B –

17

a *major seventh*. Aside from the perfect fourth and fifth, all of these are major intervals. These give to the major scale its characteristically bright modal colour. Use the major scale therefore, for all upbeat, bright and cheerful pieces of music.

The Natural Minor Scale

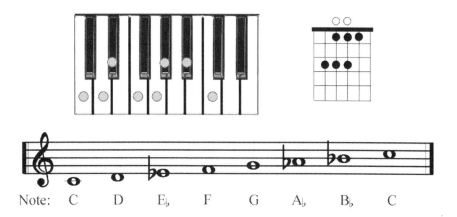

| Note: | C | D | E♭ | F | G | A♭ | B♭ | C |

Origin: European.

Scale Type: Heptatonic diatonic.

Tuning: Equally tempered.

Styles of Music: All Western styles

Transposition: 2 – 1 – 2 – 2 – 1 – 2 – 2.

Features: The natural minor scale offers a beautiful modal contrast to the major scale, one directly analogous to the difference between say, shadow in contrast to light or night in contrast to day.

Aside from the perfect fourth, fifth and the major second degree, all of the other notes of the natural minor scale form minor intervals with the tonic. These are the minor third (note E flat), sixth (note A flat) and seventh (B flat). The characteristic modal coloring of the natural minor scale is due to the presence of these minor intervals, a presence which gives to music written in the natural minor scale, a modal coloring appreciably darker than that of the major scale.

Like the major scale, the natural minor scale is used in virtually every style and genre of modern Western music. However, classical composers tended to favor the harmonic or melodic minor scales, so the natural minor scale was less often used in classical music.

The Harmonic Minor Scale

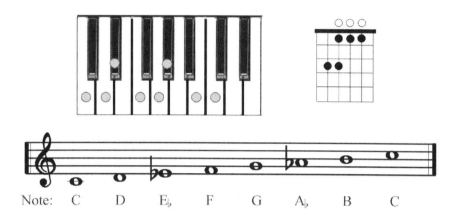

Note: C   D   E♭   F   G   A♭   B   C

Origin: European.

Scale Type: Heptatonic.

Tuning: Twelve-tone equal temperament.

Styles of Music: All Western styles.

Transposition: 2 – 1 – 2 – 2 – 1 – 3 - 1.

Features: A common variant of the minor scale is the harmonic minor scale – a scale that was used more or less exclusively in Classical music - at the expense of the natural minor scale. The difference between the natural and the harmonic minor scale lies in one feature. The seventh degree of the harmonic minor scale has been raised by a semitone. This brings the seventh degree closer to the pitch of the tonic note. Being closer, the seventh degree progresses melodically up to the tonic in a much more incisive and conclusive way. However, by raising the seventh degree of the natural minor scale in this way, an augmented second scale step is created between the notes A flat and B. This can give to the harmonic minor scale a distinct Turkish or Moorish feel.

The Melodic Minor Scale

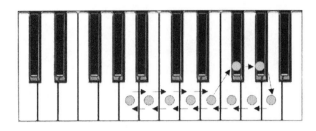

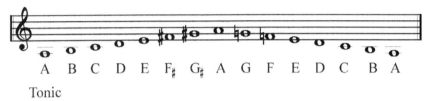

A   B   C   D   E   F♯ G♯ A   G   F   E   D   C   B   A

Tonic

Origin: European.

Scale Type: Heptatonic.

Tuning: Twelve-tone equal temperament.

Styles of Music: All Western styles.

Features: In the melodic minor scale, the seventh and the sixth degrees of the natural minor scale are raised in order to enhance a sense of melodic drive upwards to the tonic note C. By sharpening the sixth, the augmented second between the sixth and seventh degrees – a conspicuous feature of the harmonic minor scale – is also eliminated. This leads to a smoother sense of stepwise motion which many classical composers greatly appreciated. On descent however, the scale reverts back to the natural minor form.

The Chromatic Scale

Note: C   D♭   D   E♭   E   F   F♯   G   A♭   A   B♭   B   C

Origin:	European.
Scale Type:	Dodecaphonic.
Tuning:	Twelve-tone equal temperament.
Styles of Music:	All Western styles.
Transposition:	I – I – I – I – I – I – I – I – I – I – I - I

Features: The chromatic scale is probably *the* most important scale of Western music. Primarily, this is because most other Western musical scales can be obtained by selecting particular notes from the chromatic scale. Examples of this are the major scale, or the natural, harmonic and melodic minor scales, all of which are contained within the twelve-note chromatic scale.

To play a rising chromatic scale on a keyboard therefore, one begins with the starting note, which can be any note on the keyboard, and then one simply touches every key on the way up until the octave of the starting note has been reached. From this it can be seen that the chromatic scale embraces all of the twelve notes in any octave of the keyboard. For this reason, the chromatic scale is more rarely used as a musical scale in its own right, composers preferring instead to select say five, six or seven notes out of the total range of twelve notes that are available. Selections of five notes are called *pentatonic scales*, six notes *hexatonic scales* and seven notes *heptatonic scales*.

Notes which fall outside of the chosen scale may of course be used by a composer. These extra notes are generally understood as being chromatic notes, resulting from the chromatic embellishment of a melody written within a particular scale. A good example of this is the Bebop Major scale, which is an ordinary major scale to which a chromatic passing note has been added between the fifth and sixth degrees. In the key of C, as featured below, this passing note appears as a G sharp:

The Bebop Major Scale

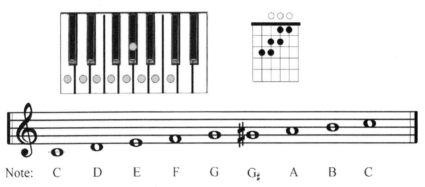

| Note: | C | D | E | F | G | G♯ | A | B | C |

As this passing note is a regular feature of Bebop practice it therefore becomes integral to the scale itself.

In classical terms, a distinction is often made between the melodic and harmonic forms of the chromatic scale. Although both scales are played using the same set of twelve notes, they are often notated differently. In the melodic form of chromatic scale chromatic notes are often written as sharps on ascent and flats on descent:

The Rising and Falling Forms of the Melodic Chromatic Scale

Rising: C   C♯   D   D♯   E   F   F♯   G   G♯   A   A♯   B   C

Falling: C   C♭   B♭   A   A♭   G   G♭   F   E   E♭   D   D♭   C

Where the harmonic form of chromatic scale is concerned, a tonic note is considered to be an integral feature of the scale. Each note of the harmonic form of chromatic scale thereby forms a particular interval with that tonic note. The harmonic form of the chromatic scale therefore has a defined key. In the case of the key of C, the intervals formed by each note of the chromatic scale with the tonic note C are:

Degree	Note	Interval
I	C	Unison
2	Db	Minor second
3	D	Major second
4	Eb	Minor third
5	E	Major third
6	F	Perfect fourth
7	F#	Augmented fourth
8	G	Perfect fifth
9	Ab	Minor sixth
10	A	Major sixth
11	Bb	Minor seventh
12	B	Major seventh
I	C	Octave

Knowledge of the structure of the harmonic form of chromatic scale is essential for any musician who wants to be able to understand and explore different musical scales and modes. As originally mentioned under the section preliminary concepts, this is because each note of a given modal scale will form an interval with the tonic note. This interval in its turn, will contribute to the perceived modal colour, the major and augmented intervals of the harmonic form of chromatic scale generally contributing a bright modal colour, the minor intervals a dark colour.

Because this knowledge is so important, it is recommended that every musician learn how to build a harmonic form of chromatic scale from any required keynote. This is done by methodically adding to the keynote the next step of the scale determined by its particular interval. Therefore for example if the chosen keynote is A:

- The *second step* of the scale is a minor second above the tonic, which is an interval of one semitone – in this case note B flat.

- The *third step* of the scale is a major second above the tonic, which is an interval of two semitones – in this case note B.

- The *fourth step* of the scale is a minor third above the tonic, which is an interval of three semitones – in this case note C.

- The *fifth step* of the scale is a major third above the tonic, which is an interval of four semitones – in this case note C sharp.

- The *sixth step* of the scale is a perfect fourth above the tonic, which is an interval of five semitones – in this case note D.

- The *seventh step* of the scale is an augmented fourth above the tonic, which is an interval of six semitones – in this case note D sharp.

- The *eighth step* of the scale is a perfect fifth above the tonic, which is an interval of seven semitones – in this case note E.

- The *ninth step* of the scale is a minor sixth above the tonic, which is an interval of eight semitones – in this case note F.

- The *tenth step* of the scale is a major sixth above the tonic, which is an interval of nine semitones – in this case note F sharp.

- The *eleventh step* of the scale is a minor seventh above the tonic, which is an interval of ten semitones – in this case note G.

- The *twelfth step* of the scale is a major seventh above the tonic, which is an interval of eleven semitones – in this case note G sharp.

In this way a harmonic form of chromatic scale can be methodically constructed upon any keynote that is required. When the musician has learned this scale in every key, initially following the procedure just outlined, they will then find it much easier to remember, play and use any of the scales given in this book - in any key that is required. Any time spent upon this important task is therefore never wasted.

Section 2: The Diatonic Modes

Excluding for the moment the chromatic scale, the entire repertoire of Western classical music, written between say the 17th – 19th centuries, generally uses only two basic scales. These are the major and the minor scales. An impression of greater modal diversity appears because of the use of various forms of the minor scale. However, these do not alter the fact that as far as a sense of *mode* is concerned, Western classical music was based on a dualistic system, the contrasting terms of which are major and minor.

Because of the dominance of both major and minor scales over the classical repertoire, they tend to receive a great deal of attention in the process of Western music education, where the repertoire of classical music is still preserved as an iconic model of musical value and development. In some ways, this helps to explain their pre-dominance even in Western popular music. They are scales which, due to the general influence of Western musical education, are most likely to be known to music producers and songwriters generally.

The system that uses the major and minor scales is often referred to as *the tonal system*. The most salient features of this system are the use of the major and minor scales within a scheme of key relations that allows for the building of either scale upon any degree of the twelve-tone chromatic scale. This gives rise to that $(2 \times 12 = 24)$ system of keys, a system that is still taught as the main theoretical element today when learning to play a musical instrument such as piano, violin, trumpet or oboe.

Now although the tonal system is limited in terms of the number of scales it uses, compensation for this is provided in the form of rich possibilities for modulation or movement between different keys. These give to the music a great deal of variety, as they enable the composer to take the listener on a fascinating journey through the different regions of the key system.

However, one of the prices for this system is equal temperament, a system of tuning whereby all of the semitones of the chromatic scale are given a standard size of 1/12th of the total octave space. Generally taken as the standard tuning for the instruments of Western music, important keyboard instruments such as the piano or organ are all rigorously tuned in this way. The frets on guitars are also spaced in order to produce equally tempered semitones.

As one possible form of tuning, equal temperament stands in contrast to pure tuning, also known as *just intonation*. In just intonation, each musical interval is tuned according to a whole number ratio. According with the natural modes of vibration of the strings and tubes used to make musical instruments, just intonation has always counted as a much more natural method of tuning.

However, if all of the notes of the major and minor scales, including the triads which can be built on upon each degree of the scale were tuned using just intonation, a scale of *at least* some fifty-or sixty notes per octave would be required. Moreover, many of these notes would simply be tiny scraps of a tone brought in to enable the pure tuning of say a single chord.

For this reason, the use of equal temperament in tonal music has always been seen to be very advantageous. For it allows a great reduction in the number of notes needed to play a piece of music. Imagine a piano with fifty odd keys to the octave, or fitted with a series of cumbersome pedals designed to raise or lower the pitch of particular notes by a tiny fraction. The sheer effort involved would make the performance of even the simplest piece of music very difficult indeed. Suffice to say, in many ways equal temperament can be very convenient.

Alternatives to the Major and Minor Scales

Although the major and minor scales are still in use today, they are by no means the only scales available for the process of music making. They are two out of what are potentially thousands of possible scales that could also be used, even operating within the accepted limitations of the Western twelve-tone chromatic scale. Within the bounds of the chromatic scale, there are still many different scales that composers can, do or have used, these being obtained by selecting certain of the twelve notes and excluding others.

Probably the best way of approaching a study of these alternative scales is through looking at the way in which the boundaries of the original tonal system of Western music were being continually pushed from about the second half of the nineteenth century onwards. There were many reasons for this push, one of which was a desire for originality, a wish to create new, fresh and exciting sounds.

One such direction of exploration lay in the increased use of chromaticism, which is the use of notes from outside of the major or minor scales for decorative and coloristic purposes. The use of such chromatic notes became an increasingly important feature in classical styles of music as the nineteenth century progressed. However, although this general trend towards the increased use of chromaticism did indeed lead to a great expansion of coloristic possibilities, in the end this practice began to undermine the foundations of the tonal system itself. Chords became more complex and dissonant, melodies became increasingly chromatic, and the powerful sense of tonality that had pervaded the music of previous eras began to lose its firm footing.

Once this gradual breakdown of tonal values precipitated by the use of chromaticism became apparent, a new dawn of musical experimentation ensued. A part of this was that composers not only began to question traditional tonal values, but they also commenced an exciting search for new possibilities.

Inevitably, these searches occurred in numerous different directions. One such direction was the gradual abandonment of the system of tonality itself. As tonality was becoming weakened, why not just abandon it altogether? This direction of exploration led in the end to various techniques of *atonal composition* in which all sense of a tonal centre in the music was deliberately avoided. This was accomplished through rejecting diatonic scales and adopting the twelve-tone chromatic as the main scale. Each of the twelve notes could then be treated as functional equals in order to avoid any suggestion of a tonal hierarchy. This naturally led to a redefinition of the twelve-tone chromatic scale as the *dodecaphonic scale*, a scale in which all twelve notes existed on an equal footing.

Another direction that suggested itself was the exploration of the musical possibilities of altogether new types of musical scales. Why should a composer limit himself or herself to just the major, minor or indeed the twelve-tone chromatic scale of Western tradition? Surely, other scales can be used for the purposes of musical creation.

In his *Sketch of a New Esthetic of Music* Ferruccio Busoni (1866 – 1924) gave voice to these feelings as they appeared in his own time at the early beginnings of the twentieth century. At one point in this work, he speaks about the narrowness of our tonal range, and how it has become so stereotyped that any familiar motive can now be fitted with another familiar motive.[3]

Speaking about how jaded the resources of the tonal system had become, Busoni also turned his attention to the limitations imposed by equal temperament. He observed that because of equal temperament we are no longer capable of hearing some of the finer distinctions of tone which belong to what he called an *infinite gradation*.[4]

This point made by Busoni is a good one. Between two notes an octave apart is indeed an infinite gradation, one which belies the perception of the equally tempered twelve-tone scale as being the only and only possible scale that composers could use. Theoretically, it is possible to divide the octave into any number of scale steps. Moreover, amongst these there may be scale divisions that, although unknown to us today, might provide the basis for the new music of future generations.

---

[3] Ferruccio Busoni, *Sketch of a New Esthetic of Music, p.22 - 23.*
[4] Ibid, p. 24.

Busoni then goes on to discuss the unity of the key system whereby he manages to reduce the system of twenty-four keys down to just one key. Viewing the major and minor tonalities as but two expressions of a whole, one which can be transposed eleven times, he points out that in truth our key system reduces down to a very simple unity.[5]

Evidently dissatisfied with the limitations even of this unitary tonal system, Busoni goes on to discuss how different scales might be devised and used, as he considers to have been already demonstrated in some of the works of Franz Liszt (1811 – 1886), Claude Debussy (1862 – 1918) and Richard Strauss (1864 – 1949).[6] In order to demonstrate this, Busoni describes how, through a process of either raising or lowering the various degrees of the diatonic scale many other new types of scale might be arrived at. He refers to examples such as a D flat minor scale in which note C is used as the tonic instead. Other examples he gives are scales such as:

- *C Db Eb Fb G A B C;*
- *C Db Eb F Gb A B C;*
- *C D Eb Fb Gb A B C;*
- *C Db E F Gb A Bb C;*
- *C D Eb Fb G A# B C;*
- *C D Eb Fb G# A B C;*
- *C Db Eb F# G# A Bb C.*

In presenting such scales, Busoni alludes to the wealth of melodic and harmonic expression that such novel scales would enable.[7] Without a doubt, Busoni does present here a novel range of different scales. However, he seems to have been unaware of the fact that many of the 113 scales he refers to were actually already in use, and had been in use for centuries, in the modal music of countries such as Arabia, Greece, Turkey, Iran, Afghanistan, Pakistan and India. Therefore what seemed to be exciting, fresh and new possibilities for Busoni were simply well established features of the age-old musical traditions of these countries.

---

[5] Ibid, p. 27.
[6] Ibid., p. 29.
[7] Ibid., p. 29 – 30.

In seeking a more definitive answer to the problems that he saw with the tonal system, Busoni also suggested the idea of going beyond twelve-tone equal temperament and adopting a scale of eighteen one-third tones which gives each of the sharps and flats a different pitch. In other words, Busoni felt that the answer lay not in the already well-established chromatic possibilities of the twelve-tone scale, but in the enharmonic possibilities of an eighteen-tone scale. What I mean by enharmonic therefore, is the use of melodic intervals smaller than a semitone. These are customarily called *microtones*.

Here again Busoni was perhaps also unaware that this world of enharmonic microtones has already been thoroughly explored in the modal music of the countries that I have just mentioned. Without even mentioning the music of ancient Greece, here I am referring to the Medieval seventeen tone scale of Persian music, the even more ancient 22 note shruti scale of Hindustani modal music or indeed the twenty-four note quarter tone scale of modern Arabian music. This is to say nothing of the 53-note scale used in Turkish music or the 72-note scale that provides the foundation for the modes of Byzantine chant. Recognizing such scales, which go far beyond the limits of Western equal temperament, the music of these traditions is thoroughly steeped in the use of microtones which arise when enharmonics are exploited.

The Ecclesiastical Modes

While for Busoni, a more refined scale of one-third tones represented an attractive theoretical proposition, other figures in music looked for and found viable alternatives to the major and minor scales in the antiquated system of Ecclesiastical modes that preceded them. Prior to the establishment of the tonal system composers had enjoyed the use of a system of modes which, being greater in number than the major and minor scales, offered at least a wider choice of musical and expressive possibilities.

Turning their attention to these modes, composers soon found themselves tapping into a revitalized resource for their music, directly inspired by this contact with what was seen to be an old and redundant modal tradition. Yet we should not be misled into thinking that this meant a return to the old ways. It did not mean for example, a resurrection of the old Church modal system. On the contrary, what was perhaps more important than the Church modes themselves, was the idea of modal expression, which had been informing the music of the Christian Church since its early beginnings in the Middle East.

Here we need to bear in mind that while Beethoven was composing his symphonic and monuments to the tonal system, much of the music being played and listened to throughout the rest of the world was based on the ancient and time-honored concept of modal music. Moreover, in the various countries of Europe modal music was being preserved in the sphere of folk music, the music played and practiced not in the aristocratic courts, but in the inns, taverns and market places of the ordinary folk.

To be able to appreciate this, we first need to get a clear grasp of the fundamental idea behind modal music, an idea that informs a vital living current of music, which has inspired and excited every composer and musician who has ever been exposed to it. To gain a sense of this idea it would be useful perhaps, to use an example of Western modal music as an illustration. One such example is *Boléro* (1928), by the French composer Maurice Ravel (1875 – 1937).

Displaying modal rather than tonal values, when the Bolero was first performed it was received with considerable surprise from some quarters, especially in the critical aftermath that followed subsequent performances. Bolero is a lengthy piece of music, some 17 minutes long which, very unusually for a piece of that length, did not significantly modulate or change key. On the contrary, the tonic note together with its fifth was continually sounded in an ostinato pattern bass line throughout the entire 17 minutes of the track. This kept the music firmly rooted in a perceptible sense of tonic led values, which offered a solid anchor for the upper melodic parts.

The melodic style was also unusual. Rather than developing organically from nuclear motifs, instead the melody was continually repeated, thereby circling around itself, and a great deal of repetition was used to emphasize certain key notes of the mode. These included the flat seventh and ninth, approached progressively as the melody ascended, in terrace like fashion, towards the higher registers. This gradual process of ascent we might note, is one of the strong characteristics of Andalusian and Arabic styles of modal music generally.

As the melody was repeated, an increase of intensity was accomplished through Ravel's deft orchestration. His intention in this respect was made clear when, playing the theme with one finger to his friend Gustav Samazeuilh he spoke of his intention to simply repeat it a number of times without any development, using instead the forces of the orchestra to engender a sense of gradual culmination.[8] This idea of repeating the theme without development is all part of modal music, for in doing so, the music creates a cumulative feeling in the listener.

While Bolero undoubtedly betrays the influence of the Andalusian style of modal music as still practiced in the Maghreb today, modal music throughout the world shows many of the traits that Ravel employed in the Bolero. The primary emphasis is always on colour, atmosphere, mood, feeling and an overwhelming sense of transcendence, a transporting of the listener to a higher, more mysterious world of myth and imagination, where anything may or could happen.

To accomplish this, repetition is used to firmly establish the modal idea in the listeners mind. Once established, the intensity of the idea can then be enhanced by whatever means are available to the musician or composer. This can be by way of a series of tempo changes, orchestration, the exploration of the idea through modulations to related modes, etc. Whatever techniques are used, the modal idea itself can offer a powerful and inspiring vehicle for musical expression.

---

[8] Arbie Orenstein, *Ravel: Man and Music*, p.98.

The Seven Diatonic Modes

Having briefly touched upon the idea of modal music, let us now see how this translates into practice. The main modes in use today are those that loosely bear a relationship to the old system of Ecclesiastical modes. I say loosely, because modern music has reinvented the modal system to suit its purposes. Therefore, the relationship of particular modes to the modes of the church is not always faithfully preserved. Some of the modes have been kept, while others that the Church might have rejected have been retained.

To appreciate this modern system of diatonic modes, recall that both major and minor scales can be derived from the same basic diatonic gamut, the difference between them being where the tonic is placed. Therefore, if we take that gamut as being represented by say, the white keys of the piano, then the major scale will take note C for the tonic, while the minor scale will take note A. In today's modal system, we find that any note of the gamut can be taken to be the prospective tonic. This means that as well as building individual scales whose tonics are note C (major scale) and A (minor scale) respectively, it is also possible to take say note D to be the tonic, or note G, and so on.

Each of these individual scales is called a *mode*. Moreover, as the original diatonic scale has seven notes, this means that there are in theory at least, seven possible diatonic modes. Each of these modes bears a name, the names themselves originating from the music of ancient Greece. Then the modes were named after particular tribes of people, whose general character was felt to be reflected in the mood or ethos of the mode.[9] The names of these seven modes, together with the notes that they use are:

---

[9] This issue of assigning Greek names to the modes has always been fraught with problems. First, the modes are ascribed different Greek names to the originals. Second, the Greek names themselves often tended to refer to particular styles of music, rather than scales of notes. Two modern equivalents of this are the Hungarian minor scale associated with Roma music and the Spanish Phrygian mode associated with Flamenco. Note that both national tags have stylistic associations.

The Seven Diatonic Modes

Degree:	I	II	III	IV	V	VI	VII	VIII
Ionian:	C	D	E	F	G	A	B	C
Dorian:	D	E	F	G	A	B	C	D
Phrygian:	E	F	G	A	B	C	D	E
Lydian:	F	G	A	B	C	D	E	F
Mixolydian:	G	A	B	C	D	E	F	G
Aeolian:	A	B	C	D	E	F	G	A
Locrian:	B	C	D	E	F	G	A	B

Looking at this group of modes a number of important features present themselves.

- All seven modes can be obtained from the same group of seven notes. These are the seven indicated by the seven letters of the musical alphabet: C D E F G A B, i.e. the white keys.

- The modal tonic is indicated by the first degree of each mode. Therefore, each mode has a different tonic note. The Ionian mode has tonic note C, the Dorian mode tonic note D and so on.

- Different modes are obtained by simply rotating the tonic – that is shifting up or down the scale.

In this sense, the diatonic modal system has a very simple basis. There is one basic scale of seven notes, which then yields seven separate modes through a process of tonic rotation. Of the seven, two correspond to the major and minor scales of classical traditions. These are the *Ionian mode*, which corresponds with the major, and the *Aeolian mode*, which corresponds with the minor. It therefore becomes apparent that the majority of diatonic modes did not survive the transition from the modally based music of earlier periods to the tonally based music of the later classical periods.

The essential differences between these modes lie in the particular sequence of scale step sizes that they offer. We can appreciate this if we represent the seven modes in a circular format, in which the scale step sizes are represented as arcs of the circle, a tone being signified by T and a semitone by S:

The Seven Diatonic Modes Represented in Circular Format

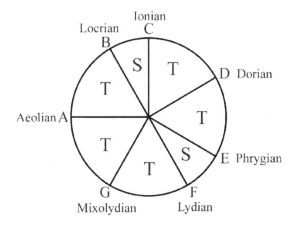

Here we can see that while the Ionian mode offers the sequence of scale steps T T S T T T S, the Dorian offers a different sequence, which is T S T T T S T. In addition, we will see that with each mode, not only do the semitones occur at different points, but also the augmented fourth interval between notes F and B is differently placed. The placing of this augmented fourth interval is a crucial feature of each of the modes. This is because it is the only augmented fourth present in the entire gamut. All of the other fourths are perfect fourths.

Because of what was perceived to be its sinister sound, this interval received the appellation of 'Devil's Fourth' in the Middle Ages. However, this term does not really do any justice to the fact that the augmented fourth represents one of the crucial features of the diatonic modes in general. This is because the augmented fourth is a powerful dissonance. Being dissonant it represents a powerful source of tension and instability within each of the modes, each of the notes of the augmented fourth tending to pull in opposite or conflicting directions. As this sense of conflict is differently placed in each mode, this greatly contributes to the character and definition of each mode.

Because each of the modes is crucially different to one another in this respect, each mode has its own particular feel, mood or colour. In fact, the word mode itself comes from the ancient Greek word for mood. When a composer writes their music in a particular mode therefore, their music can greatly benefit from the particular feel that the mode brings to the music. Moreover, when they become more experienced in modal composition, they will be able to access the various archetypes that over the ages have come to be associated with the various domains of modal expression.

These archetypes include particular elements, planets, colours, etc. – all of which represent in symbolic form the domains of the human psyche which these modes are capable of tapping into. Naturally, this implies that the modes themselves are very powerful vehicles for human emotional expression.

The Chromatic Foundation Scale

Another important feature of the modern modal system is that a composer does not necessarily feel any sense of constraint to write their music within a particular mode. They may choose to as the case may be. However, the modes themselves are simply a number of available choices, amongst an entire array of choices that are available to them. These choices include the seven diatonic modes, which are the subject of this chapter, but they also include much else besides. We have already observed that Busoni enumerated 113 possible seven-note scales which composers are all free to use should they choose. Moreover, this is only taking into account seven note scales. When scales with two, three, four, five, six, seven, eight, nine, ten, eleven and twelve notes are brought into the mix the number of choices a composer has are astronomical.

Because of this large number of choices available to modern composers, it is always advantageous to work from a scalar home base, this home base being the twelve-tone chromatic scale. From this scale, the composer will then select the notes they need for the purposes of their composition. This may turn out to be all twelve, seven, five or even only a few. Therefore, for example if a composer produces music which turns out to be in the Dorian mode, they will clearly select some of the notes of the chromatic scale but not necessarily others.

For this reason, it is convenient to view the diatonic modes as being particular selections of notes from the chromatic scale. However, in order to do this, it is first necessary to group the modes in a certain way. All of the modes need to be transposed so that they will have a common modal tonic note. This modal tonic note will be the first degree of each mode.

The Seven Diatonic Modes Transposed into the Key of C

Degree:	I	II	III	IV	V	VI	VII	VIII
Lydian:	C	D	E	F♯	G	A	B	C
Ionian:	C	D	E	F	G	A	B	C
Mixolydian:	C	D	E	F	G	A	B♭	C
Dorian:	C	D	E♭	F	G	A	B♭	C
Aeolian:	C	D	E♭	F	G	A♭	B♭	C
Phrygian:	C	D♭	E♭	F	G	A♭	B♭	C
Locrian:	C	D♭	E♭	F	G♭	A♭	B♭	C

Now as the chromatic scale has twelve notes, this means that any one of these twelve can be chosen to be a modal tonic. The chromatic scale as such offers the possibility for twelve possible modal tonic notes. Naturally, this represents a radical departure from the previous scheme whereby the modes were obtained by rotating the tonic. In this case, the tonic remains static while the scale rotates.

Working within the tonality of C therefore, the composer can choose any of these seven modes for the purposes of their composition. Representing and arranging the modes in this way also helps us to discern the essential differences between the seven modes. Therefore, we can see that the notes of the Lydian mode are all natural except for the sharp fourth. By contrast, we can see that the notes of the Locrian mode are nearly all flats. Naturally, these differences are crucial for the proper recognition of each of the modes within the context of a particular key.

We can also see that when all of the notes required to be able to play these modes with a common modal tonic of C are added up, we do indeed find that a full chromatic scale is needed. This scale is the *harmonic form of the chromatic scale*. In the table that follows each of the seven modes are shown, together with the notes of the harmonic form of the chromatic scale of the key of C that they each use.

Representing the modes in this way, we can clearly see how each mode involves a process of selection from the total number of notes in the chromatic scale. The individual properties of these selections are features which every musician and composer will find to be quite fascinating. For this reason, the modes as presented in the following table have been placed in a particular order.

- On the far left is the Lydian mode, which has a major second, third, sixth and seventh degree, as well as a sharp fourth. These all give to the Lydian mode a particular brightness of expression.
- Next is the Ionian mode where the sharp fourth has now been flattened – the note F sharp is now an F.

- The Mixolydian mode comes next where we can see that the seventh – note B – has become flattened to note B flat, indicated in blue.
- The Dorian is the same as the Mixolydian except for the third, which has become flattened from E to E flat.
- Next is the Aeolian mode where the sixth – note A, has now also become flattened to produce note A flat.

41

- In the Phrygian mode, the second has also been flattened.
- In the Locrian mode, every note is a flat except for the fourth. In this final case therefore, all of the intervals are as close to the tonic as they can be. This gives the Locrian mode a particularly dark or grave expression, which is in complete contrast to the acuteness of the Lydian mode, which lies at the opposite end of the modal spectrum.

Modes as Selections of Notes from the Harmonic Form of the Chromatic Scale

Degree	Note	Lydian	Ionian	Mixolydian	Dorian	Aeolian	Phrygian	Locrian
1	C	X	X	X	X	X	X	X
2♭	Db						X	X
2	D	X	X	X	X	X		
3♭	Eb				X	X	X	X
3	E	X	X	X				
4	F		X	X	X	X	X	X
4♯	F♯/G♭	X						X
5	G	X	X	X	X	X	X	
6♭	A♭					X	X	X
6	A	X	X	X	X			
7♭	B♭			X	X	X	X	X
7	B	X	X					
8	C	X	X	X	X	X	X	X

A Spectrum of Modal Colour

The significance of this order is that it shows that the Lydian mode is the brightest mode of the group, and as we go from left to right across the table, the modes get progressively darker or graver in expression. This change occurs one note at a time as we progress from mode to mode. The Locrian mode having six flats is therefore the darkest mode of all, as shown in the following illustration:

Scale of Seven Modes from Bright to Dark

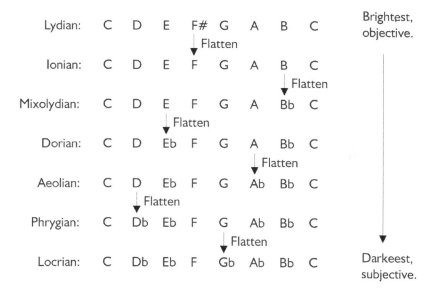

Composers have often used such schemes to assist in their creative and expressive choices. A good example of this is the American composer Roy Harris (1898 – 1979) to whom a mode was felt to be dark when its notes lay nearer to the tonic and bright when its notes lay further away. Therefore for him, the Locrian mode with its abundance of dark minor intervals was the darkest, while the Lydian mode with its abundance of bright major intervals was the brightest.[10]

---

[10] Nicolas Slonimsky, *Roy Harris*, p. 17.

Because of these obvious contrasts of modal colour, it can be convenient sometimes to think of modes in terms of specific colour associations. A commonly used association is the seven colours of the solar spectrum which, beginning with the brighter colours at the red end of the spectrum gradual transform into the darker, more somber colours at the violet end of the spectrum. This provides a good parallel to the scheme of seven modes, which range from the ultra-bright to the infra dark.[11]

The basis for this comparison is therefore self-evident. The Lydian as the brightest mode connects with the colour red, the Locrian the darkest mode with the colour violet. If these colours are then taken as being symbolic reflections of the different nuances of human emotion, we can see that the seven modes as a group thereby offer a complete range and spectrum of emotional expression from the brightest to the darkest. As such, the correlation with the colours of the solar spectrum is not something to be taken literally, but as a purely symbolic association.

Conceived as colours on a composer's palette, the modes then appear not as absolutes of musical expression, but as expressive colours, which can be merged, contrasted, blended and mixed, in a very fluid and flexible fashion. With regard to this sense of modal colour the Russian composer Nicolas Slonimsky (1894 – 1995) once made an important point about the Dorian mode, which is that on a psychological scale which extends from the darkest mode to the brightest, represented by the Locrian and Lydian modes respectively, the Dorian mode is neutral in its equilibrium.[12]

This in its turn shows that since the abandonment of the tonal system with its more limited modal spectrum, the principal scale of Western music should no longer be the major scale, but the Doric. Representing a point of equilibrium between the seven modes, the Doric stands at the very centre of the modal scheme. In reflection of this status, the Dorian is the only mode which when inverted, yields the same mode. When inverted all of the other modes occur in related pairs – Aeolian and Mixolydian, Phrygian and Ionian, Locrian and Lydian.[13]

---

[11] Ibid..
[12] Ibid.

Representing the modes on a hypothetical colour wheel in this fashion, we can also see that the Ionian and Aeolian – the major and minor modes of classical traditions, offer a nice contrast of modal colour, for they are virtually at opposite sides of the modal colour wheel. In this respect it is interesting to see that the Mixolydian and Phrygian, the Dorian and Lydian also form related pairs of modes which are similarly oppositely contrasted. For those who are interested in these contrasting relationships, in his book *Modal Music Composition*, the author Stephen Cormier offers a thorough discussion of the importance of these related pairs of contrasting modes in the evolution and development of modally based music.[14]

Here however, it is perhaps a paradox to see that the brightest and darkest of the modes – the Lydian and Locrian respectively, almost meet on the modal colour wheel. This shows that although appearing to be diametrically opposite in terms of their intervallic components (major and minor), the Lydian and Locrian modal complexes are closer than at first meets the eye.

This closeness is because they are the only modes that use the sharp fourth/flat fifth degree in relation to the modal tonic. This gives to both modes a special quality of tension, which a composer will always find a challenge to deal with. Another interesting feature is that if the first note of a Locrian mode is flattened, a Lydian mode is obtained. Therefore, even though the two modes seem to be only distantly related, the Lydian mode is only ever one alteration away from the Locrian mode.

The System of Eighty-four Modes

As there are seven modes, and the chromatic scale offers a complete spectrum of twelve possible tonic notes this means that in effect, the revamped modal system of modern music uses a system of eighty-four modes. For on each of the twelve notes seven modes can be built. The result is a complete and extensive modal system, which is not only rich in modal possibilities, but also tonal possibilities in terms of the

---

[13] Ibid..

[14] Stephen Cormier, *Modal Music Composition*, p. 99.

extensive range of keynotes available. This gives rise to very rich possibilities for modulation between modes and/or keys, which for any composer is undoubtedly a fascinating avenue of musical exploration.

To distinguish between the modes the name of the mode is given together with its keynote. Therefore, E flat Dorian means a Dorian mode built on the tonic of E flat, while F sharp Phrygian means a Phrygian mode built upon the tonic note F sharp. Mathematically speaking, the eighty-four mode system is a perfect and complete construction – a complete modal scheme foreshadowed only by the music of China where a similar scheme had been worked out perhaps thousands of years ago.

The Modes in Folk Music

While the old system of Church modes undoubtedly contributed to the formation of a new modal system in the last century, many composers also turned to the folk music of their own countries for both inspiration and a source of new ideas for their music. Within the sphere of folk music, modal traditions had often been preserved and kept for many generations, passed on orally through the repertoire of songs and melodies belonging to the folk traditions of those respective countries.

For many composers these traditions represented a rich vein of melodic resources, which could be used to revitalize the musical language. Naturally, these possibilities included not only a prospective way out from the perceived limitations of the tonal system, but also a way of forging a truly national voice that spoke directly to the people.

This intense study of folk music by composers of classical music led to many interesting avenues of musical exploration. Throughout Europe live and vital modal music traditions thrived, some of which used what seemed to be altogether new modes, modes that did not even belong to the diatonic system of modes that provided the foundation for the modal system of Church music. Naturally, these modes offered great opportunities for composers to create a fresh, reinvigorated sound as well as develop new ways of arranging and organizing their musical material.

Behind this movement however there also lay another motive. Due to the pressures of social change and transformation, people's ways of life were changing in many countries, often in directions that led to the gradual erosion of their native traditions. This process of erosion also tended to include that body of traditional music, which had formerly grown out of and helped to support those traditions.

As the process of transmission of this music was mainly oral, there was the real risk that many traditional melodies could simply disappear forever. Thus began in earnest a process of trying to collect these melodies and transcribe them into written notation so that could they then be preserved for posterity. Therefore, even though many composers did indeed draw a lot from those musical traditions, they also gave back to those musical traditions by ensuring their survival in at least some limited form, for the future.

In Great Britain, the composers Ralph Vaughan Williams (1872 – 1958) and Cecil Sharp (1859 – 1924) became well known for their efforts to collect and transcribe the traditional folk songs and dance tunes of their native country England.[15] Their efforts also helped to spur a revival of interest in folk musical traditions generally, because of which many folk songs and dances from England, Scotland, Ireland and Wales, which might otherwise have been lost to time, have now been recorded and/or transcribed into written notation. One of the main bodies, which now represent the focus for this work, is the English Folk Song and Dance Society.[16]

Cecil Sharp had numerous views about the scales and modes he observed being used in folk music. For him, they bore more of a resemblance to the musical scales of ancient Greek music than the modern scales that we use today.[17] Here however, it is clear that what

---

[15] Cecil Sharpe also did valuable work along these lines in the United States where he recorded and transcribed many traditional melodies from areas such as the Appalachian Mountains. In this respect, Sharpe also helped to spur a revival of interest in folk song in the United States too.

[16] Their website offers a lot of valuable information on the whole topic of traditional music. http://www.efdss.org/

[17] Cecil Sharp, *English Folks Song: Some Conclusions*, p. 36.

Sharp meant by this is that the scales used in folk music are also the scales used in traditional Church music, that is to say those scales that the Church had identified by Greek names.

Sharp also saw a wave of fresh interest in the modes on the behalf of composers, brought on by an increased awareness of the resources of folk music.[18] That folk songs do use the diatonic modes is self-evident. An obvious example is *Scarborough Fair*. In bar three of the melody from *Scarborough Fair* we can see the use of the note E flat as a returning tone figure to the second degree of the scale note D. While this would ordinarily suggest the minor mode, the A natural appoggiatura in bar seven shows us that this song has been written in the Dorian mode. Indeed, a closer examination of this melody reveals numerous interesting features of the Dorian mode. Observe that the first phrase makes use of the lower range of the mode and touches upon the minor third, while the second phrase moves up to the upper range and touches similarly on the major sixth. The melody therefore cleverly defines the mode over two phrases, each phrase focusing upon the two most important modal colour tones (those notes separated by a tritone):

Scarborough Fair

---

[18] Ibid.

While Scarborough fair makes effective use of the Dorian mode, the traditional folk song *Green Bushes* makes equally effective use of the Mixolydian mode. In the Mixolydian, the tritone is outlined between the flat seventh and major third – which thereby produces the two main modal colour tones. Observe the way in which Green Bushes emphasizes this tritonic connection between the modal colour tones that are notes E and B flat (i.e. bars 4, 6, 12 and 14):

Green Bushes [19]

Studies of the folk songs of other European countries have revealed that the diatonic modes, which were used in the folk music of Great Britain, were also used throughout Europe and beyond. Indeed, when Sharp went to the United States in the early twentieth century to record and transcribe folk melodies from regions such as the Appalachian mountain area, he also found the same modes being used there too.[20]

In this sense the reformation of the modal system was of paramount importance to the development of the Western musical language, for it not only served as a connection point to the ancient modal values embodied in the diatonic system of the Church modes, but it also offered a valuable point of connection with the living and vital musical traditions of the people. Traditions in which modal values have always been paramount.

Having considered the diatonic modes as a group, let us now consider each of the seven modes individually. We will begin by considering the Lydian mode first:

The Lydian Mode

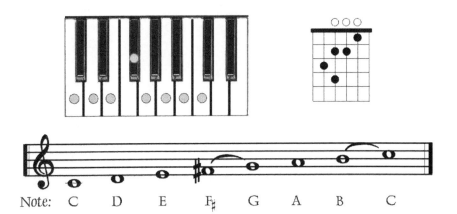

Note: C   D   E   F♯   G   A   B   C

Scale Origin: Global.

Scale Type: Heptatonic.

Tuning: Twelve-tone equal temperament.

Styles of Music: All Western styles.

Transposition: 2 – 2 – 2 – 1 – 2 – 2 - 1

Features: Because most of the notes of this mode relate to the modal tonic as major intervals, the Lydian mode counts as the brightest of the seven diatonic modes. Calculated from the key of C, these include the major second (note D), third (note E), sixth (note A) and seventh (note B). Making for a mode unclouded by any hint of a minor interval, even the fourth degree is sharp (augmented) thereby expressing a powerful acuity towards the fifth degree of the scale. It is this acuity that gives to

---

[19] Included and mentioned in Cecil Sharp and Lucy E. Broadwood's *Some Characteristics of English Folk Music*, pp. 132 – 152.
[20] Cecil Sharp's collection of melodies from this area can be found in his *English Folk Songs from the Southern Appalachians*, 2010.

the Lydian mode its perceived sense of rising upwards towards the ether, a sense that has been productively exploited by many modern composers.

Despite being generally abandoned during the Classical era, composers occasionally turned to the Lydian mode for special projects. A good example of this is Beethoven who used the Lydian mode in the third movement of his String Quartet no 15, Op. 132, entitled *Holy Song of Thanksgiving by a Convalescent to the Divinity in the Lydian Mode*. This composition was written after he had recovered from a life threatening illness. As the brightest of modes, the Lydian no doubt provided a fitting vehicle of expression for his feelings of joy and relief at having been brought back from the gates of death.

Today the Lydian mode is used in many different types of music. A particular favorite with composers of film music wishing to produce an expansive, light and buoyant atmosphere, as the brightest of modes, the Lydian lends itself well to the comic or jovial mode of expression. A good example is Dannie Elfman's theme tune to *The Simpsons*, although his use of a flat seventh in this case indicates use of a well-known variant of the Lydian mode, which musicians have named the Harmonic Lydian.

The Ionian Mode

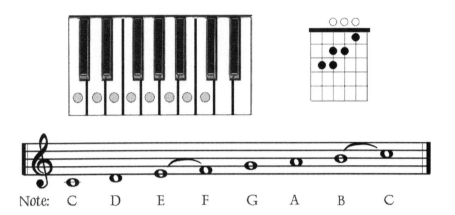

Note: C   D   E   F   G   A   B   C

Scale Origin: Global.

Scale Type: Heptatonic.

Tuning: Twelve-tone equal temperament.

Styles of Music: All Western styles.

Transposition: 2 – 2 – 1 – 2 – 2 – 2 – 1

Features: If the sharp fourth of the Lydian mode is lowered by a semitone, we get the Ionian mode. Out of the seven diatonic modes the Ionian is probably the most well known. This is because it is identical with the major scale. As such, the Ionian or major mode probably counts as *the* principal scale of Western classical music.

The Ionian mode has an interesting history. Because the Ionian tended to be used in bawdy and lustful songs, the original system of church modes did not include the Ionian mode. Acquiring epithets such as "wanton mode", the Ionian clearly acquired a reputation for use in songs that touched upon the erotic. Here it is interesting to note that the Ionian mode was aligned by Renaissance astrologers with the planet Venus, the classical Goddess of sensuality and love. It is interesting in this respect, to see that in the popular music of today, more or less dominated by such themes, the Ionian counts as a firm favorite amongst songwriters.

The Mixolydian Mode

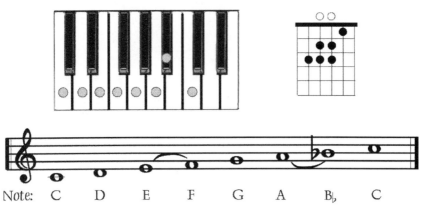

Note: C   D   E   F   G   A   B♭   C

Scale Origin: Global.

Scale Type: Heptatonic.

Tuning: Twelve-tone equal temperament..

Styles of Music: All Western styles.

Transposition: 2 – 2 – 1 – 2 – 2 – 1 – 2.

Features: When the seventh of the Ionian mode is lowered by a semitone the result is the Mixolydian mode. The Mixolydian mode therefore strongly resembles the Ionian, the difference lying in the characteristic flat seventh of the Mixolydian – a feature also shared with the Dorian, Aeolian, Phrygian and Locrian modes.

The Mixolydian is probably one of the most commonly used diatonic modes in every single style of music. In terms of classical scores, the Italian composer Ottarino Respighi's *Concerto in Modo Misolidio* (1925) represents a thorough exploration of the Mixolydian mode, from the grandeur of the first movement, to the stateliness of the theme of the slow movement and the vigor of the finale.

The flat seventh of the Mixolydian mode combines distinctively with the major third to create a mix of major and minor modal color which gives to the Mixolydian mode much of its general character. This flat seventh is an integral feature of many popular Mixolydian tunes, the song *Norwegian Wood* by the Beatles being a good example. However, the choruses of *Norwegian Wood* ingeniously switch to the Dorian mode, which means that the song as a whole employs an effective modal contrast between the brighter Mixolydian verses and the darker Dorian choruses.

Sometimes the Mixolydian mode is referred to by musicians as the 'rock scale' due to its common use in that genre of music.

The Dorian Mode

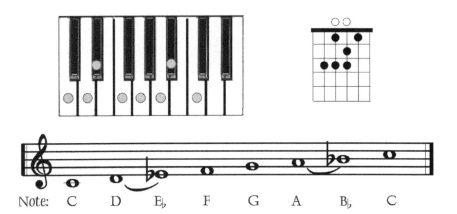

Note: C   D   E♭   F   G   A   B♭   C

Scale Origin: Global.

Scale Type: Heptatonic.

Tuning: Twelve-tone equal temperament..

Styles of Music: All Western styles.

Transposition: 2 – 1 – 2 – 2 – 2 – 1 - 2

Features: With the Dorian mode, we reach the mid-point in the scale of modal colour, a point of perfect equilibrium between darkness and bright, the former arising from the minor third and seventh degrees, and the latter from the major second and sixth degrees. *Symphony no. 6 in D Minor*, Opus 104 (1923) by the Finnish composer Jan Sibelius offers a thorough exploration of the possibilities of the Dorian mode. In this respect, Sibelius' tag of 'D minor' is misleading. Although described as being in "D Minor", this particular symphony could be more accurately described as being in D Dorian.

The Dorian is very popular in every single style of music, particularly folk and pop. Just think of Simon and Garfunkel's *Scarborough Fair* (1966) and you will get the idea.

Modern film scores often use the Dorian mode. A good example is the score to the film American Beauty (1999), whose main theme was later remixed into a very successful house track by Jakarta *American Dream* (2000). Moby's *Why Does My Heart*, part of his 1999 album *Play* makes effective use of the Dorian mode (in the key of A), revealed by his use of a repeating four chord progression: Am - Em - G major - D major.

The Aeolian Mode

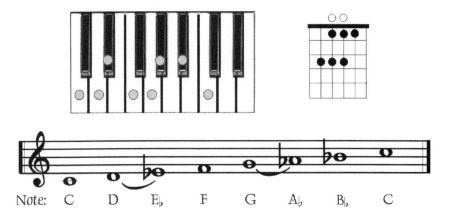

Note: C   D   E♭   F   G   A♭   B♭   C

Scale Origin: Global.

Scale Type: Heptatonic.

Tuning: Twelve-tone equal temperament

Styles of Music: All Western styles.

Transposition: 2 – 1 – 2 – 2 – 1 – 2 - 2

Features: The Aeolian mode is the modal precursor to the Western minor mode. Sharpening the seventh of the Aeolian mode for example, produced the harmonic minor mode. The Aeolian mode itself therefore corresponds to the natural minor mode in its original unaltered form - a mode still used to great effect in all styles of modern music.

A beautiful modern example of music in the Aeolian mode is the piano solo *Fur Alina* (1976) by Estonian composer Arvo Part (b. 1935). Written in the B Aeolian mode, no trace of a sharp seventh suggestive of the harmonic minor is present whatsoever. Instead, the music preserves the essential modal character of the natural minor scale (Aeolian), which lies in the flat seventh, sixth and third.

The Phrygian Mode

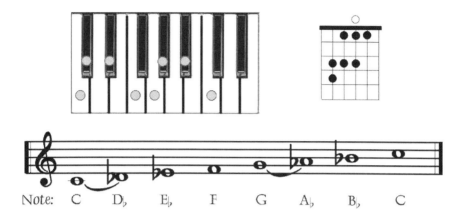

| Note: | C | D♭ | E♭ | F | G | A♭ | B♭ | C |

Scale Origin: Global.

Scale Type: Heptatonic.

Tuning: Twelve-tone equal temperament.

Styles of Music: All Western styles.

Transposition: 1 – 2 – 2 – 2 – 1 – 2 - 2

Features: To arrive at the Phrygian mode simply flatten the second degree of the Aeolian mode. Once flattened, every main modal interval of the Phrygian mode is now minor in relation to the tonic. This includes the second, third, sixth and seventh. Yielding one of the darkest and most somber of the modes, the Phrygian is rarely used in some of the lighter genres of popular music. There again, the psy-trance style of modern dance music makes the flat second of the Phrygian mode its own signature. Early styles of techno too, made great use of this flat second.

The Phrygian mode is commonly associated with Spanish Flamenco music due to its prominent use in that style. Characteristic of this style is use of the chord on the flat second degree as a substitute for the regular dominant chord.

A notable classical work that explores the possibilities of the Phrygian mode is the English composer Ralph Vaughan-Williams' *Fantasia on a Theme by Thomas Tallis* (1910), based on a melody in the Phrygian mode *"Why Fumeth in the Fight"*, originally composed by Thomas Tallis (1505 – 1585). A more modern classical work in the Phrygian mode is Wim Merten's piano solo *Close Cover* (1986).

The Locrian Mode

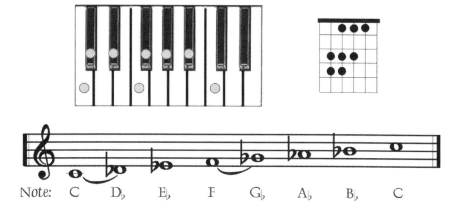

| Note: | C | D♭ | E♭ | F | G♭ | A♭ | B♭ | C |

Scale Origin: Global.

Scale Type: Heptatonic.

Tuning: Twelve-tone equal temperament.

Styles of Music: All Western styles.

Transposition: 1 – 2 – 2 – 1 – 2 – 2 - 2

Features: The seventh and final mode of the group of diatonic modes is the Locrian mode. Relative to the tonic, every single modal degree of the scale forms a minor interval. Coupled with this is the dark sounding diminished fifth degree, making for the darkest mode of the entire group of seven diatonic modes.

Very little music been written in the Locrian mode because it is not generally user friendly to Western styles of music. Mainly this is because of the diminished fifth, which does not yield a consonant triad on the modal tonic. In effect, this makes the Locrian mode difficult to handle.

One way composers have dealt with this problem is to raise the fifth degree of the mode in order to yield a useable minor triad. Otherwise, the diminished fifth is retained. When altered in this way the Locrian mode offers unique materials for composition, which many composers *have* readily exploited in their works. These materials are generally based around explorations of the tritone axis between the modal tonic and diminished fifth. In this context, the triad on the flat fifth degree is often used as a substitute for the regular dominant triad.

As one of the darkest of modes, modern styles of music have wasted no time in taking advantage of the dark brooding atmosphere produced by the Locrian mode. Heavy metal styles of rock music are often discernibly Locrian in their harmony, although again, this harmony is often based around a tritone axis between the roots of regular chords. Play the chord of B minor followed immediately by F major and you will get the sense of this.

Some of the darker and harder styles of modern dance music such as drum and bass or hard dance also make great use of the Locrian mode. These styles often use minimal tonal materials that do not rely or depend upon the use of traditional harmony. Consequently, such styles are much freer to use scales which are avoided in traditional harmony

Another use of the Locrian mode is in jazz, where the diminished tonic triad poses no problems. This is because jazz scales are often generated in response to the chords used. In an environment where dominant sounding harmonies prevail, the Locrian mode offers a perfect vehicle for melodic improvisation.

Section 3: Synthetic Modes and Scales

The diatonic modes, as considered in the last section, offered composers refreshing alternatives to the major and minor scales of Western classical music. Realizing that there were such alternatives, it was not long before composers began to experiment with these modes. This era of experimentation happened to coincide with a powerful wave of nationalism in music.

Looking to the music of their own native countries for inspiration, Western composers uncovered a literal treasure trove of traditional myths, legends, folk tales and melodies which, representing the collective inheritance of the people of that land, thereby represented the true voice of the people. Incorporating elements of these into their music thereby enabled composers to develop a truly national voice. This included composers such as Jan Sibelius of Finland, Carl Nielson of Denmark, Janacek of Czechoslovakia, Bartok and Kodaly of Hungary, Vaughan Williams and Gustav Holst of England, Albeniz and Manuel de Falla of Spain and so on.

The national melodies of these countries often used simple diatonic modes. This included melodies in say the Mixolydian, Dorian or Phrygian modes. They also included melodies, which suggested intriguing variations of these basic modal colours. A good example of this is the well known folk song *Saucy Sailor* from Cecil Sharpe's Somerset collection of folk melodies where it is listed as number 92. In the 1970's Steeleye Span made an electric-folk arrangement of this traditional song which then went on to become a hit.

The Saucy Sailor

The final note G suggests this to be an air in the Mixolydian mode centered on G. However, the occurrence of note E flat in bar three suggests that the mode being used in this melody is a Mixolydian mode with a chromatically flattened sixth. Alternatively, the very same mode could be construed as being an Aeolian mode with raised third. Evidently this mode confused Sharp for he wrote that it is obviously not a diatonic mode and that he had never come across an air in this scale before, or indeed, knew of one discovered by any other collector.[21]

However, in his studies of some of the parallels between modal structures used in both Eastern and Western European folk music, Lajos Vargyas observed that although unknown to Sharp, the Mixolydian mode with flat sixth was commonly used in Moravian, Hungarian and Rumanian folk music.[22]

This example highlights the fact that folk music all over Europe and beyond did not confine itself simply to the diatonic modes. Numerous interesting variants of these modes were also in use. Ostensibly, these appeared to be diatonic modes in which one or more notes had been chromatically altered – that is raised or lowered to alter the profile of the mode.

There is no doubt that some of these altered modes originated from lands outside of Europe, such as countries of the Middle East, India, Japan and China. Yet whatever their origin, along with the original diatonic modes themselves, it is clear that such modes provided a new

---

[21] C. Sharp & C. L. Manson, *Folk Songs from Somerset*, no. 92.
[22] L. Vargyas, *Some Parallels in Modal Structures in Western and Eastern Europe*, p. 22.

and exciting resource for musical composition.

Obtaining New Modal Colours

In terms of the inherent logic behind chromatically altering certain degrees of a mode, we can observe that a diatonic mode has seven notes. For the purposes of obtaining variations of a given diatonic modal colour, three of those degrees tend not to sustain alterations without radically transforming the original mode itself. These are the tonic and the two main modal colour tones as outlined by the modal tritone.

To alter the tonic is pointless because the tonic is the foundation for the mode itself. Altering the main modal colour tones (as defined by the tritone) is also pointless, as this will generally turn the mode into another diatonic mode. Indeed, it is often only the presence of these modal colour tones, as we will soon see, that enables the mode itself to be properly identified.

The diagram below illustrates this logic with reference to the Mixolydian mode on G:

Potential Chromatic Alterations of Mixolydian Scale Degrees

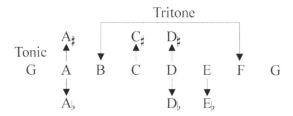

Looking at this diagram it is easy to see that, excluding the modal core provided for by the tonic and the tritone, other degrees of the Mixolydian mode can in effect, be raised or lowered by a semitone in order to create interesting Mixolydian variants. The variant used in Saucy Sailor of course, uses one of these possible options in which the sixth of the mode has been flattened.

That being said, there are some modes which either tend to defy categorization of this sort, or else hover ambiguously between diatonic modal categories. These latter tend to be modes which, like the Mixolydian mode with flattened sixth just mentioned, harbor two or more tritones. This brings them into the range of more than one diatonic mode.

Synthetic Scales

Given that diatonic modes *can be* chromatically altered and transformed, composers also tried developing their own scales and modes, which could be used either for the purposes of a particular composition, or on a more broad basis as one of the distinguishing features of their musical style. In this context belong modes, which are often named after composers that used and devised them, or prominent musical works in which they were featured. This includes for example, Alexander Scriabin's hexatonic 'Prometheus scale' or indeed the so-called 'Shostakovich scale' – both of which will be discussed in the scales menu that belongs with this section.

In Western musical theory these modes are often referred to as being *synthetic scales* – although I am not completely sure why - for they are often no more synthetic than the diatonic modes themselves. Whether considered synthetic or otherwise, these chromatically altered modes have since become an important feature of modern Western compositional practice. For which reason, they represent an undeniable contribution to the musical scales of the world.

Names for Synthetic and Alternative Scales

Each of the modes shown and discussed in the scales menu belonging to this section will be ascribed the name by which musicians most commonly know them. However, bear in mind that these names are often a hotchpotch of different terms that have no real logic behind them. Sometimes in fact, they can be completely misleading. A good example of this is the so-called 'Spanish Phrygian' – a mode that is no more Spanish than any other mode. Indeed, the very same mode is known as *Ahavah Rabbah* in the Klezmer music of Eastern Europe, and

Hijaz in the folk music of Greece. Bearing this in mind, we need to realize that these names are often no more than convenient tags.

Names commonly given to some of these modes also tend to mix up tonal and modal nomenclature. Good examples of this are the major and minor Locrian modes whose terms of reference derive from two sources – one, the tonal system with its use of the words *major* and *minor* and two, the modal system with its use of the word *Locrian*. As such, these names are again simply convenient identifying tags.

Acoustic Scale

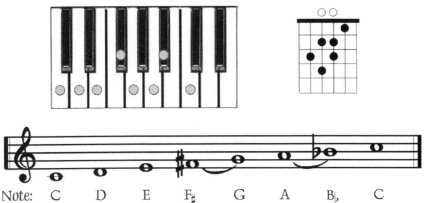

Note:	C	D	E	F♯	G	A	B♭	C

Scale Origin: East European.

Scale Type: Heptatonic.

Tuning: Twelve-tone equal temperament.

Styles of Music: Western styles.

Transposition: 2 – 2 - 2 - 1 – 2 – 1 - 2

Features: The acoustic scale is a variant of the Lydian mode in which the seventh has been flattened. An alternative method of creating the acoustic scale is to sharpen the fourth of the Mixolydian mode. As such, the so-called *acoustic scale* mixes modal colours belonging to both Lydian, with its characteristic sharp fourth and Mixolydian with its flat seventh.

The acoustic scale is also sometimes called the Lydian dominant scale, due to the prominent dominant seventh chord on the first degree (C E G Bb). The presence of this chord can give Lydian dominant music a powerful sense of unresolved dominant tension. When persistently denied resolution, this tension can be harnessed to create a powerfully expressive force.

Another name given to this scale is the harmonic Lydian. Both appellations *acoustic* and *harmonic* refer to the fact that the intervals formed by each scale degree with the tonic all suggest prominent overtones of the fundamental tone or tonic. These include:

- the perfect fifth (note G) suggesting the third harmonic;
- the major third (note E) suggesting the fifth harmonic;
- the flat seventh (B flat) suggesting the seventh harmonic;
- the major second (note D) suggesting the ninth harmonic;
- the augmented fourth (F sharp) suggesting the eleventh harmonic;
- the major sixth (note A) suggesting the thirteenth harmonic.

The terms acoustic or harmonic as applied to this scale, therefore suggest that the acoustic scale is naturally implied by the harmonic series. To find out more about this particular feature of the scale it is necessary to study acoustics, where the harmonic series is a very important phenomenon. Although the study of acoustics falls outside of the scope of this book, some independent research in this area, conducted on behalf of the musician will bring great benefits. This research should proceed to the point where the musician can work out the notes of the harmonic series from any given fundamental tone.

Numerous twentieth century classical composers made good use of the acoustic scale, amongst which were Franz Liszt (1811 – 1886), Claude Debussy (1862 – 1918), Igor Stravinsky (1882 – 1971) and Béla Bartók (1881 – 1945). The latter used it so prominently that the acoustic scale is now sometimes simply called the Bartók scale.

A popular modern melody written in the acoustic scale is Danny Elfman's theme tune to the *Simpsons* cartoon series.

Hungarian Major I

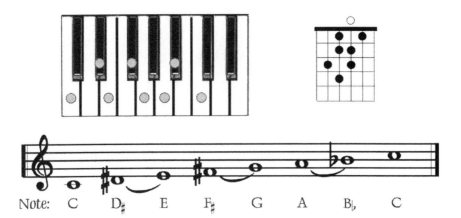

Note: C   D♯   E   F♯   G   A   B♭   C

Scale Origin: East European.

Scale Type: Heptatonic.

Tuning: Twelve-tone equal temperament.

Styles of Music: All modern styles.

Transposition: 3 – 1 – 2 – 1 – 2 – 1 - 2

Features: The name Hungarian major stems from the perceived popular use of this scale in the folk music of various East European countries. The Hungarian major scale raises the second and flattens the seventh degree of the Lydian mode. As such, the Hungarian major mode resembles an acoustic scale, the second of which has been chromatically raised. The sharp second and flat seventh bring the Hungarian major into the range of two diatonic modes – the Lydian mode with its characteristic sharp fourth and the Mixolydian mode with its flat seventh. This produces a mode with a very distinctive and unique modal colour.

Hungarian Major II

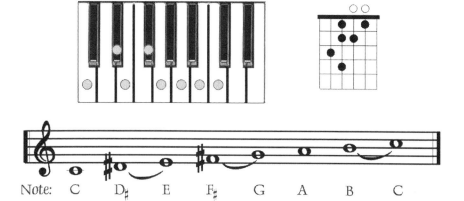

Note: C   D♯   E   F♯   G   A   B   C

Scale Origin: East European.

Scale Type: Heptatonic.

Tuning: Twelve-tone equal temperament.

Styles of Music: All modern styles.

Transposition: 3 – 1 – 2 – 1 – 2 – 2 – 1.

Features: This scale is an alternative form of Hungarian major scale in which only the second degree of the Lydian mode has been raised. Commonly used in East European music, the two forms of Hungarian major scale are sometimes fused, the natural seventh being used in the ascending form, where a leading note is required up to the tonic, the flat seventh being used in the descending form.[23]

---

[23] K. Krilov, *Harmony in Bulgarian Music*, PhD Thesis, University of Oregon; p. 66.

Lydian Minor

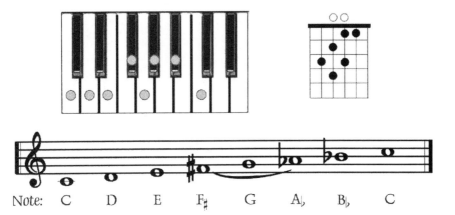

Note: C   D   E   F♯   G   A♭   B♭   C

Scale Origin: Western.

Scale Type: Heptatonic.

Tuning: Twelve-tone equal temperament.

Styles of Music: Modern styles, particularly jazz.

Transposition: 2 – 2 – 2 – 1 – 1 – 2 – 2.

Features: The Lydian minor flattens both sixth and seventh of the original Lydian mode. It is popularly called the Lydian minor due to the minor sixth and seventh degrees, which are identical with those found in the natural minor scale (Aeolian). This mode has proved itself useful in jazz for improvisations over a dominant seventh chord. When the fifth is omitted, the whole tone scale results, a scale uniquely composed of six successive whole tones.

Prometheus

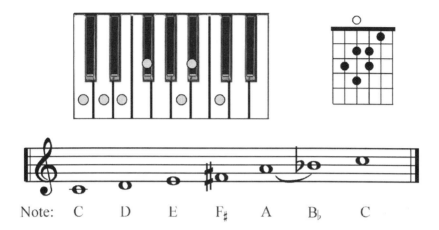

Note: C   D   E   F♯   A   B♭   C

Scale Origin: Russian.

Scale Type: Hexatonic.

Tuning: Twelve-tone equal temperament.

Styles of Music: Russian classical (original).

Transposition: 2 – 2 – 2 – 3 – 1 – 2.

Features: The 'Prometheus scale' is an artificial hexatonic or six-note scale devised by Russian composer Alexander Scriabin (1872 – 1915) for use in numerous important works such as *Prometheus: The Poem of Fire*, a work for piano and orchestra composed in the first decade of the twentieth century. In similarity with some interpretations of the acoustic scale, the notes of the Prometheus scale suggest prominent overtones of a given fundamental tone. The only difference is the omission of the fifth – note G.

For Scriabin this scale possessed a great mystic and theosophical significance deriving from its felt capability of evoking in the mind the mystic stillness of the *pleroma* – a theosophical term denoting the spiritual source of manifestation.

In more realistic terms, this scale conveys an unrelenting sense of unresolved dominant tension. This tension is due to the aural perception of the Prometheus scale as an unresolved chord of the dominant thirteenth (C E - B♭ D F♯ A).

Neapolitan Prometheus

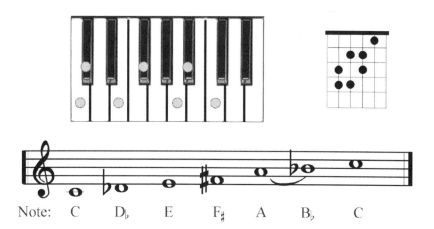

Note: C   D♭   E   F♯   A   B♭   C

Scale Origin: Russian.

Scale Type: Hexatonic.

Tuning: Twelve-tone equal temperament.

Styles of Music: Russian classical (original).

Transposition: 1 – 3 – 2 – 3 – 1 - 2

Features: The Neapolitan Prometheus scale is an alternative form of Prometheus scale developed by Russian composer Alexander Scriabin (1872 – 1915). In the Neapolitan form, the second has been flattened.

The tag Neapolitan is popularly used for modes that feature a flattened second. This term originated as a descriptive name for the chord built on the flat second degree of either major or minor scale - often used in classical music as an important pre-dominant chord. As such, the Neapolitan triad simply acted as a substitute for the regular subdominant.

Offering a powerful opportunity for use of a flat second degree within the context of the major and minor scales – where it is conspicuously absent – the name Neapolitan was later brought over to describe this flattened second scale degree within a broader modal context. Hence the name Neapolitan Prometheus which signifies the original Prometheus scale but with a Neapolitan second.

Enigmatic Scale

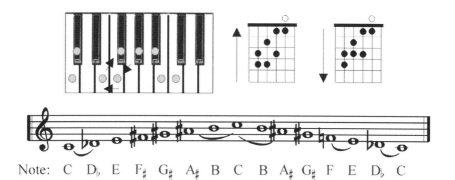

Note: C D♭ E F♯ G♯ A♯ B C B A♯ G♯ F E D♭ C

Scale Origin: Italian.

Scale Type: Heptatonic.

Tuning: Twelve-tone equal temperament.

Styles of Music: Experimental.

Features: The enigmatic scale is very much a curiosity, putting it clearly into the camp of synthetic or artificial scales. In 1888, the *Milan Musical Gazette* challenged any composer to harmonize this so-called *Scala Enigmata* – the scale illustrated.

In response to this challenge, the composer Giuseppe Verdi (1813 – 1901) composed a choral work *Ave Maria* (1888), using the outline of this scale as a cantus firmus. Although Verdi placed no significant artistic value on this work, considering it to be simply an exercise in the use of an artificial scale, it has since become one of his most popular and often-performed choral works!

Leading Whole-Tone Scale

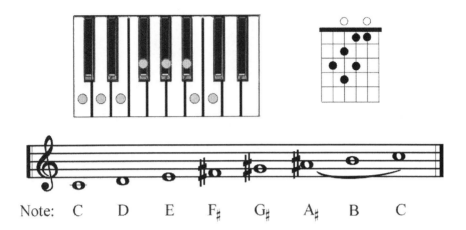

Note: C   D   E   F♯   G♯   A♯   B   C

Scale Origin: Western.

Scale Type: Heptatonic.

Tuning: Twelve-tone equal temperament.

Styles of Music: Modern classical, jazz.

Transposition: 2 – 2 – 2 – 2 – 2 – 1 – 1.

Features: The leading whole-tone scale sharpens the fifth and sixth degrees of the Lydian mode. This produces a scale where every note seems to be straining upwards to the octave of the tonic. Consequently, this scale allows for use of the whole tone scale, which by nature is tonally very vague, in a much stronger tonal context. This is assisted by the presence of a strong leading note B, which rises up nicely to the implied tonic C.

Lydian Diminished

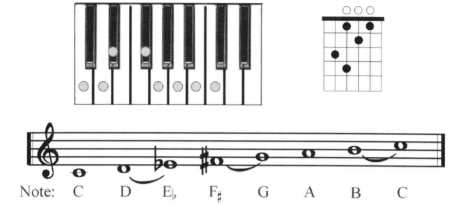

Note: C   D   E♭   F♯   G   A   B   C

Scale Origin: Russian.

Scale Type: Heptatonic.

Tuning: Twelve-tone equal temperament.

Styles of Music: Russian folk.

Transposition: 2 – 1 – 3 – 1 – 2 – 2 – 1.

Features: The Lydian diminished scale is a result of flattening the third of the Lydian mode. Due to this minor third, the Lydian diminished comes across as being a minor type mode. However, all of the other intervals are characteristically Lydian. Popularly used in the Russian peninsula of Kamchatka, numerous folk airs from this region employ this very distinctive mode.

Harmonic Major

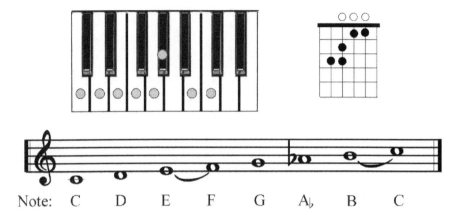

Note: C   D   E   F   G   A♭   B   C

Scale Origin: Western classical.

Scale Type: Heptatonic.

Tuning: Twelve-tone equal temperament.

Styles of Music: All styles.

Transposition: 2 – 2 – 1 – 2 – 1 – 3 – 1.

Features: The harmonic major mode flattens the sixth of the Ionian (major) mode. This creates an augmented second in the upper tetrachord (the top four notes of the scale), which resembles the upper tetrachord of the harmonic minor mode. Hence, the name usually ascribed to this mode.

The harmonic major mode changes the tonic triad of the harmonic minor scale into a major triad. This creates an interesting mixture of both major and minor modal traits. Eastern European folk music calls this scale Suzinak, resembling as it does the Turkish makam of that name.

Major-Minor Scale

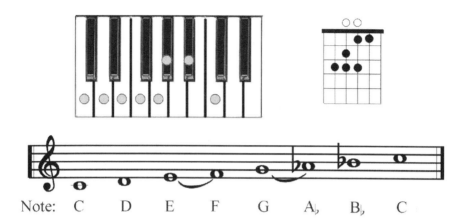

Note: C   D   E   F   G   A♭   B♭   C

Scale Origin: Various.

Scale Type: Heptatonic.

Tuning: Twelve-tone equal temperament.

Styles of Music: Various.

Transposition: 2 – 2 – 1 – 2 – 1 – 2 – 2.

Features: The major-minor mode flattens the sixth and seventh of the Ionian mode, thereby creating an interesting hybrid mode in which the lower pentachord (group of five notes) of the scale is major (Ionian) while the upper tetrachord is minor (Aeolian). This produces a fascinating mix of major and minor modal colours which many composers have found to be particularly intriguing.

Neapolitan Major Scale

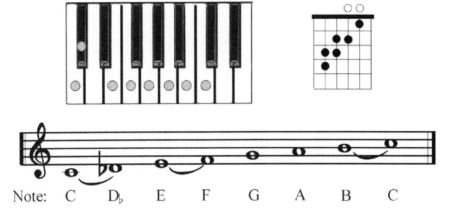

Note: C   D♭   E   F   G   A   B   C

Scale Origin: Europe; Middle East

Scale Type: Heptatonic

Tuning: Twelve-tone equal temperament

Styles of Music: Various

Transposition: 1 – 3 – 1 – 2 – 2 – 2 - 1

Features: The Neapolitan major mode flattens the second of the major (Ionian) mode. The term Neapolitan is generically used to refer to a flat second-degree effect – named after the Neapolitan triad of classical harmony. The augmented second in the lower tetrachord gives this scale its Middle Eastern flavor.

Neapolitan Mixolydian

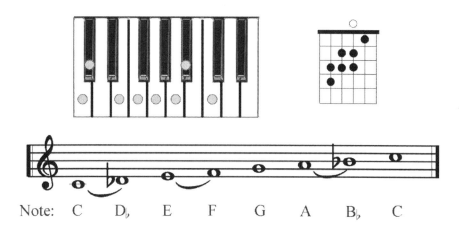

Note: C   D♭   E   F   G   A   B♭   C

Scale Origin: East European; Middle Eastern.

Scale Type: Heptatonic.

Tuning: Twelve-tone equal temperament.

Styles of Music: Various.

Transposition: 1 – 3 – 1 – 2 – 2 – 1 – 2.

Features: Some of the folk music of Eastern Europe flattens the second of the Mixolydian mode. This creates an augmented second between the second and third degrees which makes this mode similar to certain makam modes used in some East European countries.

These often carry the tag of Hijaz, a generic term used in East European music for modes with an augmented second between the second and third scale degree. Bulgarian folk music often flattens the sixth of this mode on descent.[24]

Mixolydian Flat Sixth

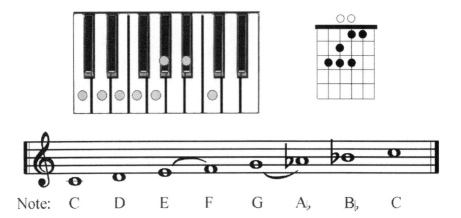

Note: C   D   E   F   G   A♭   B♭   C

Scale Origin: European (East).

Scale Type: Heptatonic.

Tuning: Twelve-tone equal temperament.

Styles of Music: Various.

Transposition: 2 – 2 – 1 – 2 – 1 – 2 – 2.

Features: The English folk air *Saucy Sailor* uses this mode, a result of . flattening the sixth of the Mixolydian mode. This mode is also known as the major-minor mode due to is major lower tetrachord and minor upper tetrachord.

---

[24] K. Krilov (2009) *Harmony in Bulgarian Music*, PhD Thesis, University of Oregon; p. 9.

Mixolydian Sharp Second

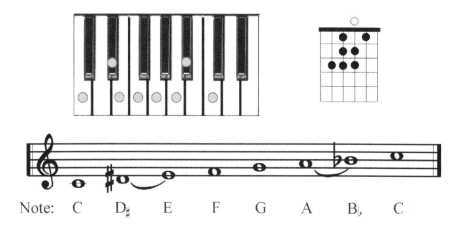

Note: C   D♯   E   F   G   A   B♭   C

Scale Origin: Various.

Scale Type: Heptatonic.

Tuning: Twelve-tone equal temperament.

Styles of Music: Jazz; blues.

Transposition: 3 – 1 – 1 – 2 – 2 – 1 – 2.

Features: A blue feel is created by the sharp second of this mode, which is then reinforced by the presence of the flat seventh. The dominant seventh chords on both first and fourth degrees – important in the blues style, define this scale in its entirety.

Otherwise, salient chords in this mode are the major/minor tonic triad, which offers great opportunities for contrast between major and minor chordal colours, together with the major triads on the sharp second degree (spelled D# G Bb) and fourth degree (F A C).

Ukrainian Dorian Mode

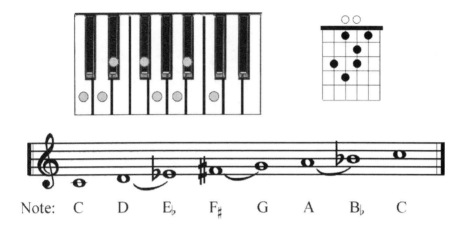

Note: C   D   E♭   F♯   G   A   B♭   C

Scale Origin: Eastern European; Greek.

Scale Type: Heptatonic.

Tuning: Twelve-tone equal temperament.

Styles of Music: Classical; folk; Klezmer.

Transposition: 2 – 1 – 3 – 1 – 2 – 1 – 2.

Features: Sharpening the fourth of the Dorian mode produces the Ukrainian Dorian mode. This is a very popular Dorian variant in Eastern Europe and the Caucasus.

The sharp fourth gives this mode a powerful driving energy – which is used to great effect in styles of music such as Klezmer, where this mode is called Doina, or the Greek folk style of Rebetiko where the same mode is called Souzenak. This latter tag relates the Ukrainian Dorian to the camp of Turkish *makam* modes.

Neapolitan Dorian

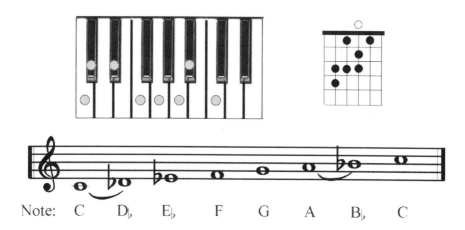

Note: C   D♭   E♭   F   G   A   B♭   C

Scale Origin: Spanish.

Scale Type: Heptatonic.

Tuning: Twelve-tone equal temperament.

Styles of Music: Various.

Transposition: 1 – 2 – 2 – 2 – 2 – 1 – 2.

Features: The Neapolitan Dorian mode is a result of flattening the second degree of the Dorian mode. Note that a Dorian mode with flat second is identical to a Phrygian mode with raised sixth. The flat second gives this mode its distinct Spanish feel.

Hungarian Minor Mode I

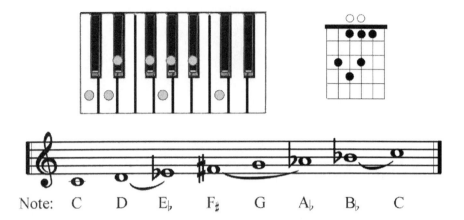

Note: C   D   E♭   F♯   G   A♭   B♭   C

Scale Origin: East European.

Scale Type: Heptatonic.

Tuning: Twelve-tone equal temperament.

Styles of Music: Various.

Transposition: 2 – 1 -3 – 1 – 1 – 2 – 2.

Features: When the fourth of the Aeolian mode is sharpened this creates an augmented second between the third and fourth degrees of the scale. This sharp fourth gives the mode its characteristic feel. Sometimes called the Magyar, Hungarian minor or Gypsy minor scale, the Russian composer Rimsky-Korsakov (1844 – 1908) used this mode in the opening theme to his *Scheherazade* (1888).

Hungarian Minor Mode II

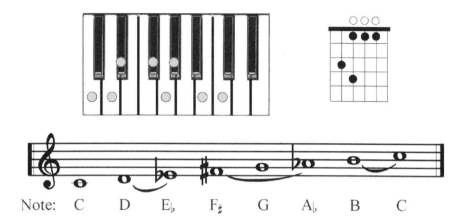

Note:	C	D	E♭	F♯	G	A♭	B	C

Scale Origin: Eastern European.

Scale Type: Heptatonic.

Tuning: Twelve-tone equal temperament.

Styles of Music: Various.

Transposition: 2 – 1 – 3 – 1 – 1 – 3 – 1.

Features: The Hungarian minor mode was first popularized by the nineteenth century composer Franz Liszt in his series of *Hungarian Rhapsodies*. Although assumed by Liszt to be used in the folk music of his native Hungary, both forms of Hungarian minor mode were more particularly used in the music of the various Roma bands, which often provided entertainment in local taverns. Hence, the title "Gypsy scale" sometimes ascribed to it.

Franz Liszt's godchild, Hungarian born pianist and composer Francis Korbay (1846 – 1913) referred nonetheless to this scale as *the* "Hungarian scale". While composers and musicians tend to place great value upon the musical qualities of these scales, the wisdom of referring to them as Hungarian, Gypsy, Magyar or whatever, is therefore questionable.

When the composers Zoltan Kodaly (1882 – 1967) and Béla Bartók (1881 – 1945) undertook an extensive collection of Hungarian folk music melodies during the early part of the twentieth century they amassed thousands of folk melodies that as a body, demonstrated the great richness and diversity of the folk music of their native Hungary.

However, they did not find any particular evidence for the use of scales that, like the Hungarian minor, tended to use augmented seconds. Consequently, Bartok came to believe that such scales probably derived from Arabic sources introduced by way of Roma music.

Here it is interesting to discover that this same mode is also used in Greek folk music where it is referred to as *Niaventi*. This name clearly betrays the influence of Turkish makam.

Seven-Tone Spanish Phrygian Mode

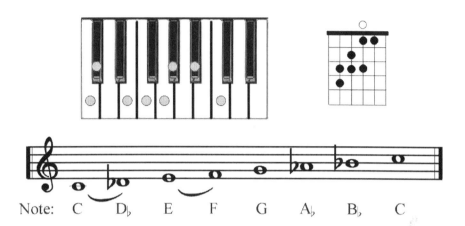

Note: C   D♭   E   F   G   A♭   B♭   C

Scale Origin: Spanish.

Scale Type: Heptatonic.

Tuning: Twelve-tone equal temperament.

Styles of Music: Flamenco.

Transposition: 1 – 3 – 1 – 2 – 1 – 2 – 2.

Features: The Spanish Phrygian mode raises the third of the Phrygian mode. This acknowledges the typical and characteristic use of a major tonic triad in Spanish folk music within an otherwise minor coloured modal environment. The Spanish Phrygian is only effective when the ear can be persuaded that the tonic triad is not the dominant of a harmonic minor scale whose tonic lays a fourth above. This is generally accomplished by treating the triad on the flat second degree as a substitute dominant, with chord vii as its back up and support. This produces the characteristic formula of the Phrygian cadence, which avoids all traces of a conventional dominant to tonic chord progression.

Eight-Tone Spanish Phrygian

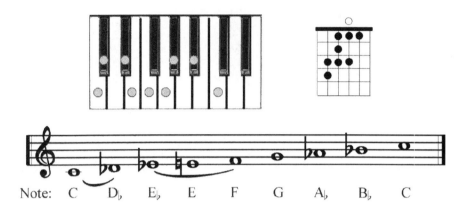

Note: C   D♭   E♭   E   F   G   A♭   B♭   C

Scale Origin: Spanish.

Scale Type: Octatonic.

Tuning: Twelve-tone equal temperament.

Styles of Music: Flamenco.

Transposition: 1 – 2 – 1 – 1 – 2 – 1 – 2 – 2.

Features: A popular chord progression in Flamenco styles of music is the so-called Andalusian *cadence*. This is the chord progression iv, III, II, I, the roots of each of these triads forming a stepwise progression down from the fourth. In the case of the key of C therefore, the Andalusian cadence would pass through the chords of Fm – Eb – Db – C.

This progression involves use of both Phrygian third in chord III and the raised third in the final major tonic chord. For this reason, the Spanish Phrygian mode is often thought of as an eight-note or octatonic mode, which includes both major and minor third degrees.

Espla's Scale

Note: C   D♭   E♭   E   F   G♭   A♭   B♭   C

Scale Origin: Spanish.

Scale Type: Octatonic.

Tuning: Twelve-tone equal temperament.

Styles of Music: Modern classical.

Transposition: 1 – 2 – 1 – 1 – 1 – 2 – 2 – 2.

Features: An eight-tone variation of the Spanish Phrygian scale used by the Spanish composer Oscar Esplá (1886 – 1976). Inspired by the folk music of his native country, Esplá developed a scale that sought to synthesize its essential elements. This scale has eight notes and is readily discernible as a clear expression of the Phrygian modal group.

Double Harmonic Scale

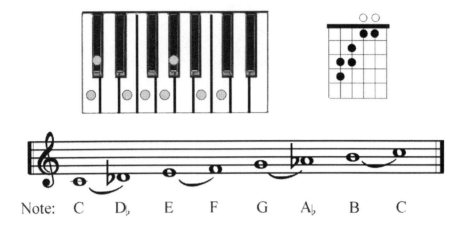

Note: C   D♭   E   F   G   A♭   B   C

Scale Origin: Oriental.

Scale Type: Heptatonic.

Tuning: Twelve-tone equal temperament.

Styles of Music: Modern classical.

Transposition: 1 – 3 – 1 – 2 – 1 – 3 – 1.

Features: When the third and seventh of the Phrygian mode are raised by a semitone the result is the double-harmonic scale – so called because of the two augmented seconds present in this scale. Representing the fifth mode of the Hungarian minor scale, the double harmonic scale has a similar feel.

In Greek folk music this mode is called Hijazkiar – which clearly relates it to the Hijaz group of Turkish makam.

Harmonic Phrygian

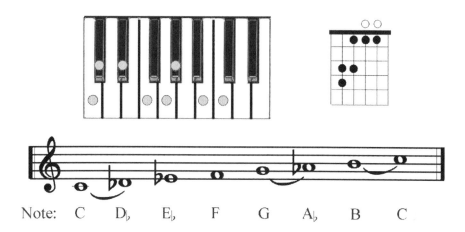

Note: C   D♭   E♭   F   G   A♭   B   C

Scale Origin: Spain; Middle East.

Scale Type: Heptatonic.

Tuning: Twelve-tone equal temperament.

Styles of Music: Modern classical.

Transposition: 1 – 2 – 2 – 2 – 1 – 3 – 1.

Features: A variant of the double harmonic scale that raises the seventh of the Phrygian mode. The flat second degree coupled with the augmented second in the upper half of the scale, gives this mode its particular Moorish feel.

Phrygian Major

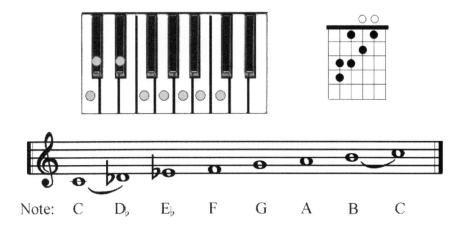

Note:	C	D♭	E♭	F	G	A	B	C

Scale Origin: Western.

Scale Type: Heptatonic.

Tuning: Twelve-tone equal temperament.

Styles of Music: Modern classical, jazz.

Transposition: 1 – 2 – 2 – 2 – 2 – 2 – 1.

Features: The Phrygian major mode, sharpens the sixth and seventh of the Phrygian mode. This produces a unique hybrid of Phrygian and Ionian modes, the lower half being Phrygian and the upper Ionian. The Phrygian major mode is non-invertible, i.e. the transposition pattern reads the same forwards as backwards.

Major Locrian

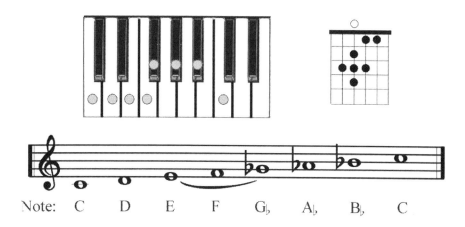

Note:	C	D	E	F	G♭	A♭	B♭	C

Scale Origin: Western.

Scale Type: Heptatonic.

Tuning: Twelve-tone equal temperament.

Styles of Music: Modern classical, jazz.

Transposition: 2 – 2 – 1 – 1 – 2 – 2 -2

Features: For what is probably one of the least used of the seven modes, the Locrian mode has spawned the greatest number of variants. This is largely due to its common use in jazz, where the Locrian mode and its various offshoots, are perfect modes for melodic improvisation over dominant harmonies such as the dominant seventh, ninth, half-diminished seventh chord and their various chromatically altered forms.

Variants of the Locrian mode can also produce crude Western versions of what is commonly thought to be Arabic, Persian and Turkish scales.

The major Locrian raises the second and third degrees of the Locrian mode by a semitone, to produce a hybrid mode consisting of an Ionian lower tetrachord and a Locrian upper tetrachord. Resulting in a scale that has five consecutive whole tones, the major Locrian is therefore linked to the leading whole tone scale, where it appears as the mode obtained in the fourth position i.e. shifting the tonic to the fourth degree.

Minor Locrian

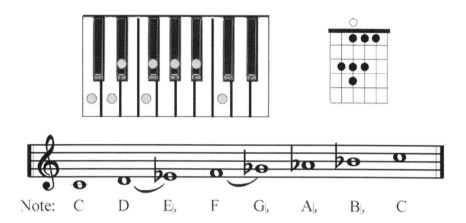

Note: C   D   E♭   F   G♭   A♭   B♭   C

Scale Origin: Western.

Scale Type: Heptatonic.

Tuning: Twelve-tone equal temperament.

Styles of Music: Modern classical, jazz.

Transposition: 2 – 1 – 2 – 1 – 2 – 2 – 2.

Features: The minor Locrian raises the second degree of the Locrian mode by a semitone. This produces a hybrid mode in which the lower tetrachord (notes C to F) is Aeolian, the upper tetrachord Locrian. In jazz, this mode is popular for improvising over the chord of the half-diminished seventh.

Locrian Minor

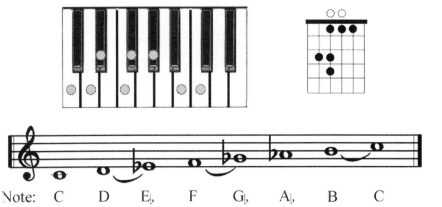

Note: C   D   E♭   F   G♭   A♭   B   C

Scale Origin: Western.

Scale Type: Heptatonic.

Tuning: Twelve-tone equal temperament.

Styles of Music: Modern classical, jazz.

Transposition: 2 – 1 – 2 – 1 – 2 – 3 – 1.

Features: The Locrian minor mode flattens the fifth of the harmonic minor scale. This again produces a modal hybrid, a composite modal colour produced by mixing the harmonic minor and Locrian modes.

Super Locrian

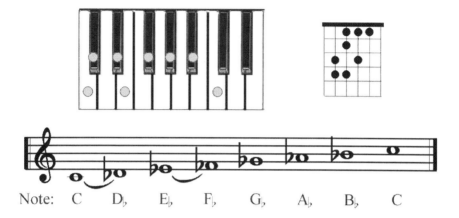

Note: C   D♭   E♭   F♭   G♭   A♭   B♭   C

Scale Origin: Western.

Scale Type: Heptatonic.

Tuning: Twelve-tone equal temperament.

Styles of Music: Modern classical, jazz.

Transposition: 1 – 2 – 1 – 2 – 2 – 2 – 2.

Features: The super-Locrian flattens the fourth of the Locrian mode. This produces a mode in which every note is being pushed as close down to the modal tonic as possible. This downwards push is the direct opposite to the upwards push of the augmented Lydian mode. Therefore, while the modal colors of the augmented Lydian and super-Locrian could not be further apart, it is interesting to see that the super-Locrian is the seventh mode of the melodic minor scale, while the augmented Lydian is the third mode – showing both to derive from the same scale complex.

Ultra Locrian

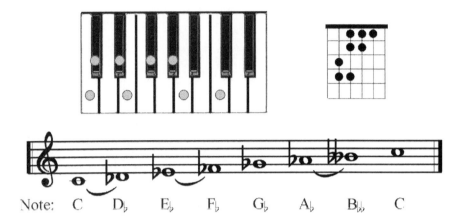

Note: C   D♭   E♭♭   F♭   G♭   A♭   B♭♭   C

Scale Origin: Western.

Scale Type: Heptatonic.

Tuning: Twelve-tone equal temperament.

Styles of Music: Modern classical, jazz.

Transposition: 1 – 2 – 1 – 2 – 2 – 1 – 3.

Features: The ultra-Locrian flattens both fourth and seventh of the Locrian mode. The ultra-Locrian goes one step further than the super-Locrian: ordinarily minor in the super-Locrian, the ultra-Locrian uses a diminished seventh obtained by flattening the already flat seventh. This produces an extremely dark modal color.

Oriental

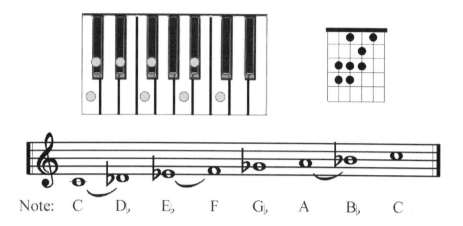

Note: C   D♭   E♭   F   G♭   A   B♭   C

Scale Origin: Middle East; Turkey.

Scale Type: Heptatonic.

Tuning: Twelve-tone equal temperament.

Transposition: 1 – 2 – 2 – 1 – 3 – 1 – 2.

Styles of Music: Modern classical, jazz.

Features: The so-called Oriental scale is a Locrian mode with a raised sixth degree, which relates it to the ultra-Locrian: while the former is the third, the latter is the seventh mode of the harmonic minor scale. The augmented second in the upper half of the octave gives this mode its typical Middle Eastern feel.

Doric Locrian

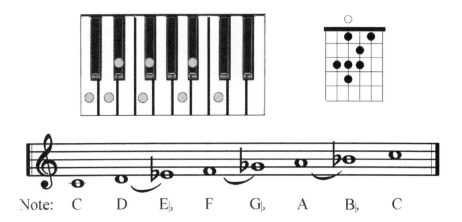

Note: C   D   E♭   F   G♭   A   B♭   C

Scale Origin: Eastern Europe; Turkey; Greece.

Scale Type: Heptatonic.

Tuning: Twelve-tone equal temperament.

Styles of Music: Modern classical, jazz.

Transposition: 2 – 1 – 2 – 1 – 3 – 1 - 2

Features: A Locrian coloring is imparted to the Dorian mode by flattening the fifth. In Eastern European music, this scale is sometimes called Karcigar, resembling as it does the Turkish makam of that name.

Persian

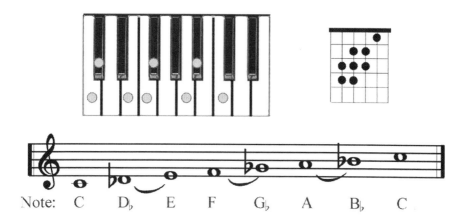

Note: C   D♭   E   F   G♭   A   B♭   C

Scale Origin: Greece; Turkey; the Middle East.

Scale Type: Heptatonic.

Tuning: Twelve-tone equal temperament.

Styles of Music: Modern classical, jazz.

Transposition: 1 – 3 – 1 – 1 – 3 – 1 – 2.

Features: The Persian mode raises the third and sixth of the Locrian mode, to result in a mode with an augmented second in both upper and lower tetrachords. For Western listeners at least, this gives the mode a distinctive Middle Eastern feel. This mode is also used in Greek folk music where it is called Tsinganikos.

Tcherepnin Enneatonic Scale

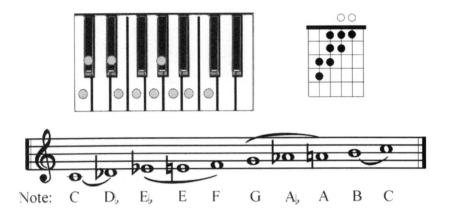

Note: C   D♭   E♭   E   F   G   A♭   A   B   C

Scale Origin: Russian.

Scale Type: Enneatonic.

Tuning: Twelve-tone equal temperament.

Styles of Music: Modern classical.

Transposition: 1 – 2 – 1 – 1 – 2 – 1 – 1 – 2 – 1.

Features: The Russian composer Alexander Tcherepnin (1899 – 1977) developed this scale for use in some of his more mature works. It has many interesting properties, including the use of both major and minor triads whose roots are the same degree of the scale.[25] Tcherepnin viewed this scale as consisting of three repeating segments of a semitone, tone and semitone.

---

[25] More information about Tcherepnin's music and his use of particular scales can be found in his *Basic Elements of My Musical Language* which is hosted on the Tcherepnin Society website which can be found here: http://www.tcherepnin.com/alex/basic_elem1.htm

Tcherepnin Hexatonic Scale

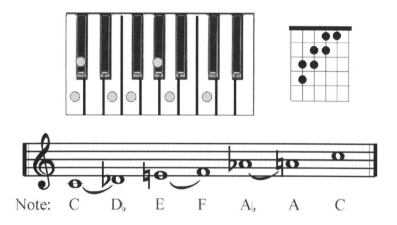

Note:　C　D♭　E　F　A♭　A　C

Scale Origin:　Russian.

Scale Type:　Hexatonic.

Tuning:　Twelve-tone equal temperament.

Styles of Music:　Modern classical.

Transposition:　1 – 3 – 1 – 3 – 1 – 3.

Features: Tcherepnin also made great use of certain subsets of his nine-note scale. One such subset is this hexatonic scale consisting of alternating intervals of a semitone and minor third/augmented second. This produces a hexatonic scale with remarkable symmetrical properties, as well as a set of major and minor triads that work beautifully together.

Shostakovich

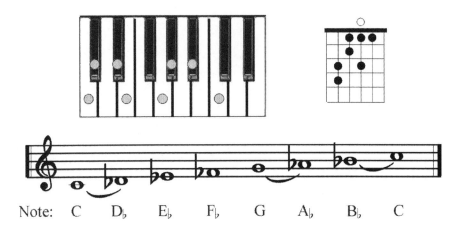

Note: C   D♭   E♭   F♭   G   A♭   B♭   C

Scale Origin: Russian.

Scale Type: Heptatonic.

Tuning: Twelve-tone equal temperament.

Styles of Music: Modern classical.

Transposition: 1 – 2 – 1 – 3 – 1 – 2 – 2.

Features: The Shostakovich scale was used in numerous works by the Russian classical composer Dmitri Shostakovich (1906 – 1975). It appears as a Phrygian mode with lowered fourth. The lowered fourth degree gives the scale a bleak, melancholic feel which Shostakovich used to great effect in works such as the Sixth Symphony (1939).

Modal Relationships

A useful area of research is exploring the relationships between the modes considered in the last few sections. Most of the modes just considered have seven notes. Now usually the first degree of the mode is the tonic. However, in practical terms we may take any of these seven notes to be a prospective tonic. Shifting the tonic in this way is called rotating the tonic.

By rotating the tonic it is possible to generate seven modes from any other mode. Generated from the same order of intervals, all of these modes are related by this fact. Accordingly, modes can be grouped in sets of seven, each group consisting of those which can be generated from a common interval sequence. Therefore, if we take the harmonic minor mode as an example (Aeolian raised seventh) and rotate the tonic the following set of seven related modes appears. Each of these modes have been transposed onto a common keynote for comparison, in this case note C:

The Seven Modes of the Harmonic Minor Scale

1st:	C	D	E♭	F	G	A♭	B	C	Harmonic minor
2nd:	C	D♭	E♭	F	G♭	A	B♭	C	Locrian 6#
3rd:	C	D	E	F	G♯	A	B	C	Ionian 5#
4th:	C	D	E♭	F♯	G	A	B♭	C	Ukrainian Dorian
5th:	C	D♭	E	F	G	A♭	B♭	C	Spanish Phrygian
6th:	C	D♯	E	F♯	G	A	B	C	Hungarian major
7th:	C	D♭	E♭	F♭	G♭	A♭	B♭♭	C	Ultra Locrian

Here therefore we can see that the Spanish Phrygian and Ukrainian Dorian are both modes of the same scale – the harmonic minor scale.

Now if the order of intervals in the harmonic minor scale are reversed (2 1 2 2 1 3 1 semitones) another related mode is obtained – its modal inversion. To obtain this inversion simply follow the order of intervals in the harmonic minor mode except proceed from top to bottom rather than bottom to top. This then produces:

Harmonic Minor Mode and Inversion

C   D   E♭   F   G   A♭   B   C   Harmonic minor

C   D♭   E   F   G   A   B♭   C   Mixolydian flat second

Each mode in a given group of seven relates to an inverted mode, thereby connecting together two groups of seven modes. In the case of the above group, this produces the following two groups of connected modes:

Modes Connected by Inversion

Mode	Inversion
Harmonic minor	Mixolydian flat second
Locrian 6#	Lydian Diminished
Ionian 5#	Phrygian 4b
Ukrainian Dorian	Doric Locrian
Spanish Phrygian	Harmonic Major
Hungarian major	Locrian 7#
Ultra Locrian	Lydian 2/5#

Among all of the modes, there are certain modes that have special properties. These are the non-invertible modes:

Non-invertible Seven Note Modes

Phrygian major:	C	D♭	E♭	F	G	A	B	C
Dorian:	C	D	E♭	F	G	A	B♭	C
Double harmonic:	C	D♭	E	F	G	A♭	B	C
Major – minor:	C	D	E	F	G	A♭	B♭	C

Composers have always found the properties of non-invertible modes to be particularly fascinating, for they are the musical equivalent of palindromes. When any melody written within such a mode is inverted i.e. played upside down, the interval structure of the melody is faithfully preserved.

Section 4: Scales of Greek Folk Music

Another group of modes that have attracted strong interest from musicians are those used in various styles of Greek folk music, in particular the very popular style of Rebetiko often heard being played live in Greek taverns. This music has a unique sound, much of which is due to the distinctive set of musical modes used by that style of music.

The modes used in Rebetiko and other related styles of Greek folk music bear a strong relationship to Turkish makam - as the names for many of these modes testify. Rast and Hijaz for example, are the names of two very popular Turkish makam. Fretless instruments such as the violin, oud, or the bouzuki fitted with extra frets, can easily play the subtle microtones required for a proper realization of Turkish makam. Makam however, are not strictly musical scales, but pre-defined melodic pathways through the notes of a particular mode. For this reason, the study of makam falls outside of the scope of this book.

Besides which, many modern Greek musicians have simply adapted the scalar content of various makam, enabling them to harmonize their modal melodies with simple chords. In order to do so, the Western equal tempered twelve-tone scale is used as a base. When played in this way, the subtleties of the microtones used by the original makam are lost. However, one advantage of this is that the melodies can then be harmonized using major and minor triads.

This process of adaption makes the scales of Greek folk music very accessible, for it means they can be played upon instruments such as the guitar and keyboard. For this very reason, the various modes of Rebetiko offer a fascinating area of study for musicians interested in exploring the scales and modes of particular musical cultures.

Hijaz

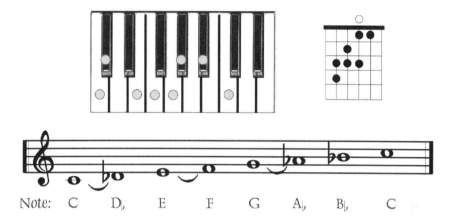

Note: C   D♭   E   F   G   A♭   B♭   C

Scale Origin: Greek.

Scale Type: Heptatonic.

Tuning: Twelve-tone equal temperament.

Styles of Music: Greek folk music.

Transposition: 1 – 3 – 1 – 2 – 1 – 2 – 2.

Features: Hijaz is a very beautiful and distinctive mode, and is immediately recognizable as the fifth mode of the harmonic minor scale i.e. the mode obtained when one adopts the fifth note of the harmonic minor scale as a tonic. The salient feature of Hijaz is the augmented second of the lower tetrachord which relates it to the Hijaz family of Turkish makam. Another way of looking at Hijaz is as a Phrygian mode the third of which has been raised by a semitone. This makes it identical with the Spanish Phrygian mode, or alternatively the popular Klezmer mode Ahavah Rabbah. Hijaz is typically used with chords built on the first, fourth and seventh degrees – very similar to the Spanish Phrygian.

113

Souzinak

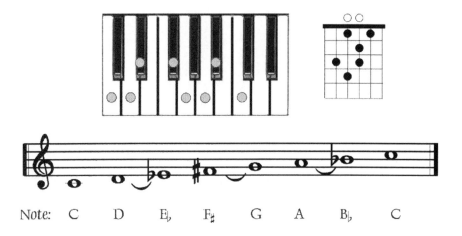

Note: C   D   E♭   F♯   G   A   B♭   C

Scale Origin: Greek.

Scale Type: Heptatonic.

Tuning: Twelve-tone equal temperament.

Styles of Music: Greek folk music.

Transposition: 2 – 1 – 3 – 1 – 2 – 1 – 2.

Features: Souzinak is a Dorian mode the fourth of which has been raised. Once raised in this way, the mode acquires a fiery quality of intense pathos. Souzinak is recognizable as the fourth position of the harmonic minor scale. This makes it identical to the Ukrainian Dorian mode, or the Doina mode of Klezmer.

Souzinak works well with chords on the first, fourth and fifth degrees.

Hijazkiar

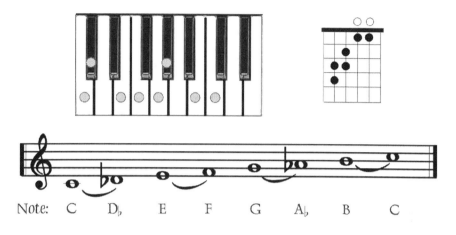

Note: C   D♭   E   F   G   A♭   B   C

Scale Origin: Greek.

Scale Type: Heptatonic.

Tuning: Twelve-tone equal temperament.

Styles of Music: Greek folk music.

Transposition: 1 – 3 – 1 – 2 – 1 – 3 – 1.

Features: Hijazkiar is notable for the augmented second in both lower and upper tetrachord. This gives it an unmistakable Middle Eastern feel. The double-harmonic mode of Western music is clearly based on Hijazkiar, a mode which is typically used with chords built on the first, second and fourth degrees of the scale.

Rast

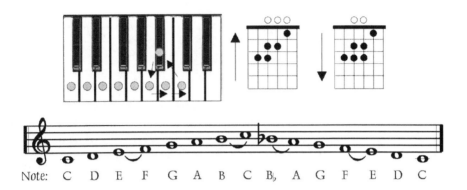

Note: C   D   E   F   G   A   B   C   B♭   A   G   F   E   D   C

Scale Origin: Greek.

Scale Type: Heptatonic.

Tuning: Twelve-tone equal temperament.

Styles of Music: Greek folk music.

Features: Rast is the Greek version of one of the most important and popular Makam of traditional Turkish music. In its ascending form, Rast is like the Western major scale, while on descent the seventh is flattened, as in the Mixolydian mode. This gives Rast a very distinctive spectrum of modal colours.

Houzam

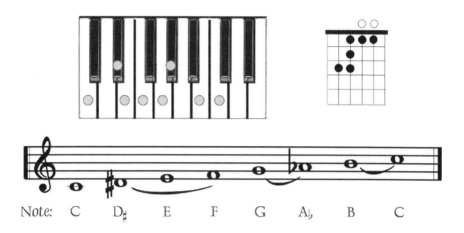

Note: C   D♯   E   F   G   A♭   B   C

Scale Origin: Greek.

Scale Type: Heptatonic.

Tuning: Twelve-tone equal temperament.

Styles of Music: Greek folk music.

Transposition: 3 – 1 – 1 – 2 – 1 – 3 – 1.

Features: Houzam is another mode with an augmented second in both upper and lower tetrachords. However, the position of the chromatic lower tetrachord is different to Hijazkiar, in that the augmented second lies between the tonic and second degree, which is then followed by two consecutive semitones. Houzam works well with chords built on the first, fourth and fifth degrees of the scale.

Ousak

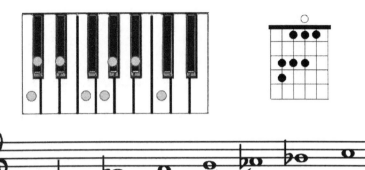

Note: C   D♭   E♭   F   G   A♭   B♭   C

Scale Origin: Greek

Scale Type: Heptatonic

Tuning: Twelve-tone equal temperament

Styles of Music: Greek folk music

Transposition: 1 – 2 – 2 – 2 – 1 – 2 – 2.

Features: Ousak is identical to the Phrygian mode. As such Ousak works well with chords on the first, fourth and seventh degrees.

Niaventi

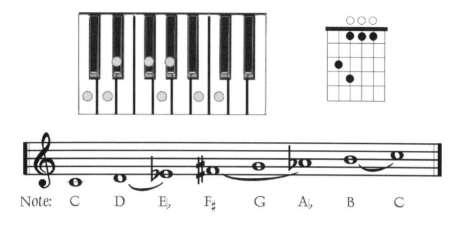

Note:	C	D	E♭	F♯	G	A♭	B	C

Scale Origin: Greek.

Scale Type: Heptatonic.

Tuning: Twelve-tone equal temperament.

Styles of Music: Greek folk music.

Transposition: 2 – 1 – 3 – 1 – 1 – 3 – 1.

Features: Niaventi is like a harmonic minor mode, the fourth of which has been raised. This makes it identical with the Hungarian minor mode. Niaventi works well with chords on the first, fifth and sixth degrees. A triad can also be used on the second degree, the fifth sometimes being raised to produce a major triad.

Kiordi

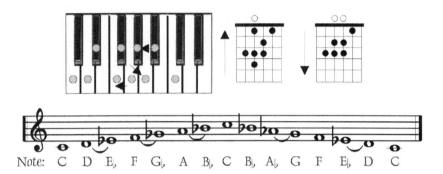

Note: C D E♭ F G♭ A B♭ C B♭ A♭ G F E♭ D C

Scale Origin: Greek.

Scale Type: Heptatonic.

Tuning: Twelve-tone equal temperament.

Styles of Music: Greek folk music.

Features: Like Rast, Kiordi has two forms, a rising form which appears as a Dorian mode with flattened fifth (Doric Locrian), and a falling form in which it is identical with the Phrygian mode. The chord on the first degree of the rising form will often raise the fifth to produce a tonic minor triad.

Tsinganikos

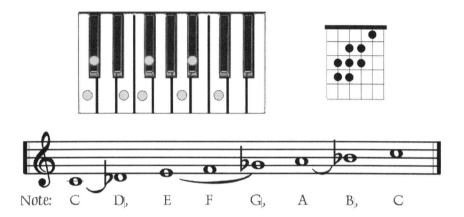

Note: C   D♭   E   F   G♭   A   B♭   C

Scale Origin: Greek.

Scale Type: Heptatonic.

Tuning: Twelve-tone equal temperament.

Styles of Music: Greek folk music.

Transposition: 1 – 3 – 1 – 1 – 3 – 1 – 2.

Features: Tsinganikos is like a Locrian mode the third and sixth of which have been chromatically raised. This gives rise to another of those modes that have an augmented second in both upper and lower tetrachords. Tsinganikos can also be obtained by beginning on the fifth degree of Hijazkiar.

Periaiotikos

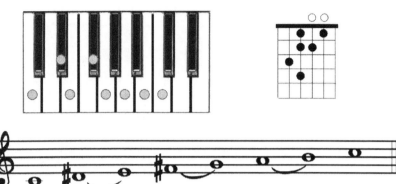

Note: C   D♯   E   F♯   G   A   B   C

Scale Origin: Greek.

Scale Type: Heptatonic.

Tuning: Twelve-tone equal temperament.

Styles of Music: Greek folk music.

Transposition: 3 – 1 – 2 – 1 – 2 – 2 – 1.

Features: Periaiotikos has the apparel of a Lydian mode with raised second. This creates an augmented second between the tonic and second degree of the mode. Combined with the sharp fourth, this makes for a very distinctive modal colour. It is identical with one of the forms of the Hungarian major mode.

Sabach

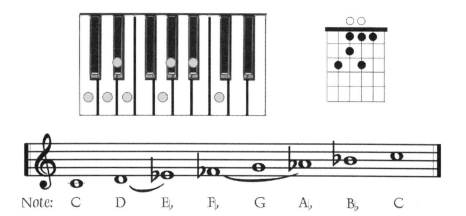

Note: C   D   E♭   F♭   G   A♭   B♭   C

Scale Origin: Greek.

Scale Type: Heptatonic.

Tuning: Twelve-tone equal temperament.

Styles of Music: Greek folk music.

Transposition: 2 – 1 – 1 – 3 – 1 – 2 – 2.

Features: Sabach is a natural minor mode the fourth of which has been flattened. This gives rise to some interesting chords, such as the augmented triad on degree four, or the major triad with flat fifth on the degree seven.

Segiah

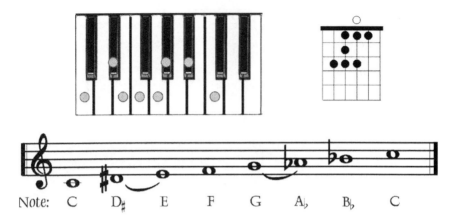

Note: C D♯ E F G A♭ B♭ C

Scale Origin: Greek.

Scale Type: Heptatonic.

Tuning: Twelve-tone equal temperament.

Styles of Music: Greek folk music.

Transposition: 3 – 1 – 1 – 2 – 1 – 2 – 2.

Features: Segiah has an augmented second between tonic and second degree in the lower tetrachord. The upper tetrachord is like the natural minor mode. Segiah works well with chords on the first, fourth and fifth degrees.

Section 5: Pentatonic Scales

In their continual search for new scales, another scale that captured the interest of composers was the pentatonic scale - a scale of only five notes that had previously been widely used in the folk music traditions of many countries, both within and outside of the reach of the Western world. Indeed, amongst all of the scales that are used in world music, the pentatonic scale counts as an indispensible article of the common musical heritage of all peoples of the world. The evidence for this is the fact that the pentatonic scale has been found in use upon every single continent of the planet Earth.

In the West, the pentatonic scale is sometimes colloquially referred to as the 'black key scale', for the simple reason that if we play only the black keys of the keyboard we will be playing in a pentatonic scale. Children of course, tend to learn to play these keys first, making their first attempts at musical improvisation pentatonic.

A great number of young children's melodies are also pentatonic, a prime example of which is the nursery song *It's Raining*. Inevitably, being much simpler than the seven-note diatonic scale, pentatonic melodies seem to be easier for young children to learn.

One of the notable features about the pentatonic scale, as anybody who confines themselves to the black keys will soon discover, is that it is impossible to get any real discord. Every single combination of notes that is played sounds euphonious to the ear. This is mainly because the scale lacks any semitones with which to clash together. This lack of semitones not only explains the euphonious sound produced by the pentatonic scale, but it also explains the feeling of staticity that comes from purely pentatonic music.

As far as Western music is concerned however, the pentatonic scale had always lurked in the shadows of the tonal system, which meant that although at times a pentatonic influence did subtly show itself in the music of various composers, nonetheless that influence was always perceived as being a secondary one, which was generally subsumed by the tonal system itself.[26]

More specific and focused use of the pentatonic scale tended to occur in a number of different directions. One such direction was the pastoral setting. A good example of this is the music with which Act IV of Grieg's *Peer Gynt* suite (1875) opens, entitled *Morning*. This is a broad and lyrical pentatonic melody written in the key of E. And it is pentatonic because although the music is in the E major key, the leading note D sharp is typically absent, while the fourth degree of the scale, note A, is reduced to a purely ornamental role. As such, this melody displays the typical signs of pentatonics, which are the characteristic omission of two otherwise important notes of a seven note diatonic scale – in this case the fourth and the seventh.

The context in which Grieg uses the pentatonic scale in this piece is to suggest a rustic, pastoral atmosphere. Using simple static harmonies to suggest rustic sounding drones, the melody is evocative of both the countryside and the music of the people who dwell there, people who have always lived in a close relationship with the land and the natural elements.

Another common use of the pentatonic scale is to suggest the exotic atmosphere of faraway lands and places, in particular the orient where the pentatonic scale always played a much more important part than it has done in the West.

An example of this is the distinct pentatonic influence which can be discerned in Gustav Mahler's symphony *Das Lied von der Erde* (*The Song of the Earth*), based on seven poems from *The Chinese Flute*, translated by Hans Bethge (1876 – 1946). Throughout this symphony, Mahler uses pentatonic melodic motifs to suggest certain referential features of Chinese musical style. The third song in particular (*Von Der Jugend*) opens with clearly delineated pentatonic scalar movement against a horn pedal point.

---

[26] Jeremy Day-O'Connell's *Pentatonicism from the Nineteenth Century to Debussy* represents an interesting study of the influence of the pentatonic scale upon nineteenth century composers, supported by many interesting examples.

Dvorak's *Ninth Symphony in E minor* (Opus 95), often referred to as the *New World Symphony*, written during his stay in the United States between 1892 – 5, makes use of the pentatonic scale in an exotic context, especially the haunting melody which features in the Largo movement played by the English horn.

A third common context for the use of the pentatonic scale is a spiritual one. Many spirituals were written using the pentatonic scale, a famous example being *Swing Low, Sweet Chariot*. As used in this context, the pentatonic scale is sometimes thought to have been brought over to America from Africa as a result of the slave trade.

A further spiritual context is suggested by Gregorian chant – the very foundations for sacred music in the West. Many of the chants, although ostensibly written within the bounds of seven note diatonic modes, are overtly pentatonic.

A good example of this is the traditional chant *Gloria a Patri*, which is written within the minor pentatonic mode on D. Completely avoiding the notes E and B, this melody has an antiquated pentatonic style, which probably goes back thousands of years.

Of the five notes of the pentatonic scale, each note can be taken to be the tonic. This gives rise to a system of five pentatonic modes, each of which is distinguished by a different pattern of scale step sizes. In this respect, we can observe that the pentatonic scale only has two such scale step sizes, the large minor third and the smaller whole tone.

The order in which these two scale step sizes occur in each mode can be seen when the pentatonic modes are depicted within a single octave cycle:

Scale Step Order in the Five Pentatonic Modes

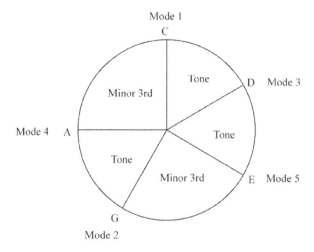

Mode 1

This figure shows that there are five pentatonic modes distinguished by the varying position of the tonic note. Depending upon where the tonic note is placed a different order of scale step sizes becomes apparent. This order in its turn, determines the intervals which each note of the scale form with the tonic. The range of these intervals in their turn, then determine the general character, colour and feel of the pentatonic mode. Nobody has ever named these modes, so they are commonly simply numbered from one to five. One such numbering system is:

The Five Pentatonic Modes

Degree:	I	II	III	IV	V	I
Pentatonic Mode 1:	C	D	E	G	A	C
Pentatonic Mode 2:	G	A	C	D	E	G
Pentatonic Mode 3:	D	E	G	A	C	D
Pentatonic Mode 4:	A	C	D	E	G	A
Pentatonic Mode 5:	E	G	A	C	D	E

As is the case with the diatonic modes, it is customary to transpose all five pentatonic modes onto a common keynote, which enables their distinct modal properties to be more easily evaluated and compared. When transposed into the key of C the five modes appear as follows:

The Five Pentatonic Modes Transposed Into the Key of C

Degree:	I	II	III	IV	V	I
Pentatonic Mode 1:	C	D	E	G	A	C
Pentatonic Mode 2:	C	D	F	G	A	C
Pentatonic Mode 3:	C	D	F	G	B♭	C
Pentatonic Mode 4:	C	E♭	F	G	B♭	C
Pentatonic Mode 5:	C	E♭	F	Ab	B♭	C

Of the five modes, two tend to be most commonly used in modern Western music. These are the major pentatonic scale corresponding to mode 1 and the minor pentatonic scale corresponding to mode 4. The frequency of their use when compared to the other modes is no doubt because in the former case, the mode is built around a tonic major triad while in the latter case, the mode is built around a tonic minor triad. Given the importance of the facility for the creation of appropriate harmonizations for melodies in Western music, it is perhaps inevitable that those modes which are the most suitable for this – the major and minor pentatonic scales – are those which have received the most attention.

Pentatonic Mode I

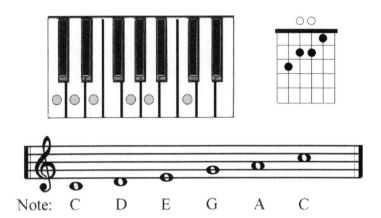

Note: C   D   E   G   A   C

Scale Origin: Global.

Scale Type: Pentatonic.

Tuning: Twelve-tone equal temperament.

Styles of Music: All styles.

Transposition: 2 – 2 – 3 – 2 – 3.

Features: The first pentatonic mode, known in the West as the major pentatonic scale, is probably the most popular and widely used pentatonic mode, featuring in classical music, folk, rock, dance, jazz and electronica in general.

The stately music which opens the movement *Morning* belonging to Grieg's *Peer Gynt Suite* (1875) is a fine example of major pentatonic melody, while another is *Auld Lang Syne*.

As the scale degrees of the major pentatonic relate to the tonic with mostly major intervals, the first pentatonic mode is consequently one of the brightest of the group.

Pentatonic Mode 2

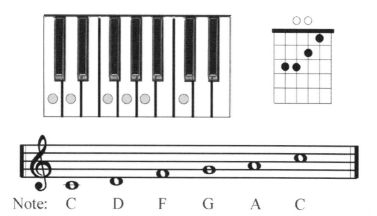

Note: C   D   F   G   A   C

Scale Origin: Global.

Scale Type: Pentatonic.

Tuning: Twelve-tone equal temperament.

Styles of Music: All styles.

Transposition: 2 – 3 – 2 – 2 – 3.

Features: In the second pentatonic mode, the major third of the first mode has been replaced by a perfect fourth. Therefore, unlike the first pentatonic mode, which strongly suggests a major triad (with added ninth and thirteenth), the second pentatonic mode suggests a 'sus.' chord, in which a fourth or second are used as substitutes for the regular third of the common triad i.e. C F G. This explains why the second pentatonic mode is sometimes referred to by musicians as the 'suspended scale'.

Pentatonic Mode 3

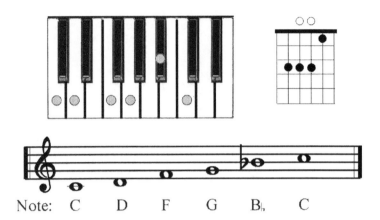

Note: C   D   F   G   B♭   C

Scale Origin: Global.

Scale Type: Pentatonic.

Tuning: Twelve-tone equal temperament.

Styles of Music: All styles.

Transposition: 2 – 3 – 2 – 3 – 2.

Features: In the third pentatonic mode, the major sixth of modes 1 and 2 has been replaced by a minor seventh. This creates a mode which is non-invertible i.e. the transposition intervals read the same going up as down. The third pentatonic mode has the same suspended quality as the second mode, except in this case, the minor seventh adds a further flavor of a suspended dominant seventh chord.

Pentatonic Mode 4

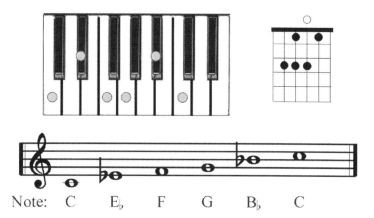

Note: C   E♭   F   G   B♭   C

Scale Origin: Global.

Scale Type: Pentatonic.

Tuning: Twelve-tone equal temperament..

Styles of Music: All styles.

Transposition: 3 – 2 – 2 – 3 – 2.

Features: After the first mode, the fourth mode is undoubtedly one of the most popularly used pentatonic modes. In the fourth mode, the major second of modes 1, 2 and 3 has now been replaced by a minor third. This gives the mode the apparel of a minor seventh chord with added eleventh (C Eb G Bb – F). It is therefore commonly called the minor pentatonic scale. The minor pentatonic has a beautiful soft mellow quality, which is used to great advantage in many different styles of music. To get an idea of this just think of Gershwin's *Summertime* or alternatively, Candy Staton's *You've Got the Love*.

Pentatonic Mode 5

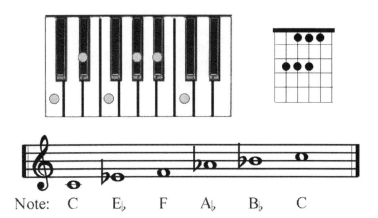

Note: C   E♭   F   A♭   B♭   C

Scale Origin: Global.

Scale Type: Pentatonic.

Tuning: Twelve-tone equal temperament..

Styles of Music: All styles.

Transposition: 3 – 2 – 3 – 2 – 2.

Features: In the fifth mode, the perfect fifth present in all of the other pentatonic modes has now been replaced by a minor sixth. This makes the fifth mode the least likely to be used in Western music. Losing the fifth, the root of any prospective tonic triad has no support. Using the sixth as a substitute creates a first inversion triad whose root is actually the sixth. This in turn undermines any sense of the true tonic. For this reason, the fifth mode tends to be impractical to use in any other context than a purely melodic one.

Section 6: Jazz Scales

The unique musical language of jazz uses many different musical scales and modes. In fact skilled jazz musicians can take any musical scale and easily adapt it to their purposes. This includes the major and minor scales of the first section, the seven diatonic modes, pentatonic modes, as well as any of the modes considered in the previous section.

This flexibility is due to the fact that jazz musicians tend to select their scales or modes according to their compatibility with the prevailing harmony. Therefore as the harmony changes, so can the scale that is used. Given a harmony such as Cmaj7 for example, then the Ionian or Lydian mode as generated from the root of that chord might be used. This is for the simple reason that the selected mode contains both the notes of the chord being used, plus any number of other notes which may be used for melodic embellishment.

This can be illustrated in the following diagram which shows the Lydian mode in C. The notes of the CMaj7 chord have been left without any fill. Observe the general compatibility between the notes of the scale and the chord itself:

Lydian Mode and CMaj7 Chord

Note: C   D   E   F♯   G   A   B   C

However, in jazz, when the chord of the song changes, a different mode may then be used. For this reason, there are a great number of scales and modes that can be used in jazz. And unlike many of styles of music which often remain within the bounds of only one scale, in jazz the scale used can change quite rapidly.

135

Although jazz can use any of the scales so far considered in this book, there are some scales which are more or less unique to the language of jazz itself and it is these which will be considered in this particular section. This includes blues and Bebop scales, developed by and for jazz musicians and scales such as jazz minor and symmetrical scales, which although originally borrowed from other styles of music are nonetheless used in very particular and distinctive ways.

The Minor Blues Scale

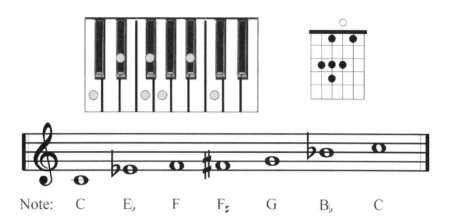

Note: C   E♭   F   F♯   G   B♭   C

Scale Origin: American.

Scale Type: Hexatonic.

Tuning: Twelve-tone equal temperament..

Styles of Music: Blues.

Transposition: 3 – 2 – 1 – 1 – 3 – 2.

Features: Blues scales are those used in the blues style of music which came to prominence in the United States during the early years of the twentieth century. Along with ragtime, the blues represents one of the important contributory styles that assisted the development of jazz through the years of the twentieth century. One of the unique contributions of blues to the global language of music is the development of a unique number of modal scales that have no real precedents elsewhere – aside perhaps for the major and minor pentatonic scales. There are two main blues scales, the minor and the major forms.

The minor blues scale is a minor pentatonic scale to which has been added a chromatic passing note between the third (note F) and fifth degrees of the scale (note G). When rising up the scale this passing note acts as an F sharp, while falling down as a G flat.

This particular note represents one of the key features that cause blues to depart from the Western classical tradition, based on the major and minor scales – neither of which prominently uses a sharp fourth/flattened fifth. This departure represented the stimulus for an entirely new branch of music generally, which has since provided the foundation for numerous popular styles of music.

The augmented fourth/diminished fifth is commonly classified as a 'blue' note. The third and seventh are also commonly referred to as 'blue' notes due to the characteristic way in which they are inflected.

The Major Blues Scale

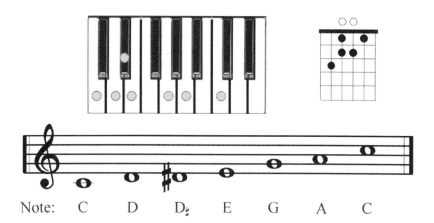

| Note: | C | D | D♯ | E | G | A | C |

Scale Origin: American.

Scale Type: Hexatonic.

Tuning: Twelve-tone equal temperament.

Styles of Music: Blues.

Transposition: 2 – 1 – 1 – 3 – 2 – 3.

Features: If we transfer the tonic of the blues minor scale onto the third note, we get the blues major scale. Built around a tonic major triad, the blues major scale has a more upbeat feel, which has been exploited in many popular styles of music from ragtime to rockabilly. Being a major pentatonic scale to which a minor third/augmented second has been added, it is the latter that gives this scale its typical blues feel.

The blues major contains both a major and a minor third. These are often combined together into one chord. This chord sounds best when the minor third is uppermost and the major third lowermost.

Bebop Dominant Scale

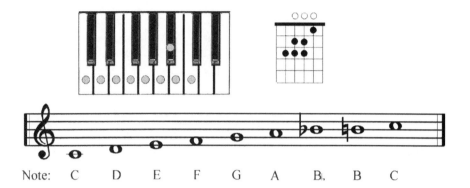

| Note: | C | D | E | F | G | A | B♭ | B | C |

Scale Origin: American.

Scale Type: Octatonic.

Tuning: Twelve-tone equal temperament.

Styles of Music: Bebop.

Transposition: 2 – 2 – 1 – 2 – 2 – 1 – 1 – 1.

Features: The style of jazz known as Bebop, associated with artists such as Charlie Parker (1920 – 1955), Dizzie Gillespie (1917 – 1993) and Hank Jones (b. 1918), first came to prominence during the years of the second world war. It then flourished through the post-war years and in doing so, laid the foundations for the practice of modern jazz as it is known of today. As a style, Bebop is generally characterized by the use of:

- a rapid, upbeat tempo

- walking bass lines

- syncopated rhythms

- use of complex chords of the ninth, eleventh and thirteenth

- a swinging eight-note rhythm

- improvised melodic lines of dazzling virtuosity

While Bebop uses a basic diatonic framework, melodies are typically embellished through use of chromatic passing notes, which do not belong to the diatonic scale. In his excellent three-volume *How to Play Bebop* David Baker observed that early 1920's jazz musicians learned to enhance the flow of their melodic lines using such chromatic passing notes.[27]

The Bebop dominant is *the* basic scale of the Bebop style. To create the Bebop dominant scale we simply take a Mixolydian mode and insert a chromatic passing note between the seventh and the eighth degrees. This converts what was a seven-note scale into an eight-note scale.

This subtle transformation is the secret to the driving forward motion, which characterizes Bebop melodies in general. This is because Bebop is typically played in swinging eighths. Because there are eight of these in a bar and eight notes in a Bebop scale, a perfect synchronization between melody and rhythm occurs, which greatly enhances the rhythmic momentum of the melodic line. This also means that, with the proviso that a chord tone is placed on one of the stronger beats of the bar (downbeats), the main chord tones of the scale always occur on downbeats too. This in turn enhances the harmonic definition of the melody.

---

[27] David Baker, *How to Play Bebop*, Vol. 1, p. 1.

Bebop Major Scale

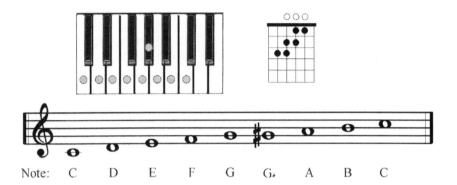

Note: C   D   E   F   G   G♯   A   B   C

Scale Origin: American.

Scale Type: Octatonic.

Tuning: Twelve-tone equal temperament.

Styles of Music: Bebop.

Transposition: 2 – 2 – 1 – 2 – 1 – 1 - 2 – 1.

Features: The major Bebop scale is a major scale to which a chromatic note has been added between the fifth and sixth degrees of the scale. As Bebop melodies are typically in swinging eighths, this conveniently places the notes of a tonic major sixth chord on the strong beats of the bar in both rising and falling stepwise motion.

In the case of the major Bebop scale, the principle chromatic note is the sharp fifth. However, there are also possibilities for the use of other chromatic notes. These include chromatic notes between the first and second, second and third, fourth and fifth, sixth and seventh.

Bebop Minor (Harmonic) Scale

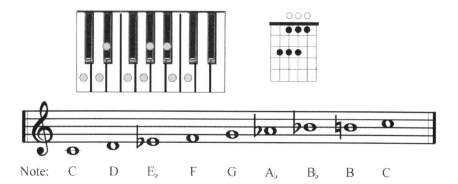

Note: C   D   E♭   F   G   A♭   B♭   B   C

Scale Origin: American.

Scale Type: Octatonic.

Tuning: Twelve-tone equal temperament.

Styles of Music: Bebop.

Transposition: 2 – 1 – 2 – 2 -1 – 2 – 1 – 1.

Features: The minor (harmonic) Bebop scale adds a passing note between the sixth and seventh degrees of the harmonic minor scale. This creates an eight note Bebop version of the regular harmonic minor mode.

Bebop Minor (Melodic) Scale

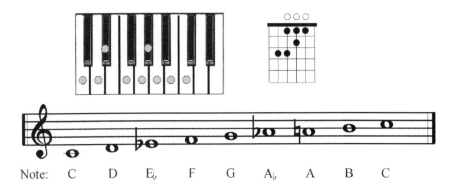

Note: C   D   E♭   F   G   A♭   A   B   C

Scale Origin: American.

Scale Type: Octatonic.

Tuning: Twelve-tone equal temperament.

Styles of Music: Bebop.

Transposition: 2 – 1 – 2 – 2 – 1 – 1 – 2 – 1.

Features: In the Bebop minor (melodic) scale, an extra note is placed between the fifth and sixth degrees to convert it into a more convenient eight note form.

Bebop Dorian Scale

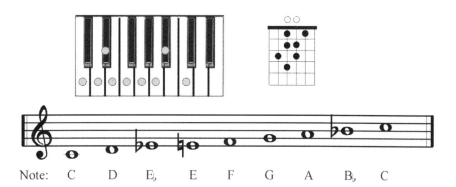

Note: C   D   E♭   E   F   G   A   B♭   C

Scale Origin: American.

Scale Type: Octatonic.

Tuning: Twelve-tone equal temperament.

Styles of Music: Bebop.

Transposition: 2 – 1 – 1 – 1 – 2 – 2 – 1 – 2.

Features: The Bebop Dorian scale is a Dorian mode to which a chromatic passing note has been added between the third and fourth degrees. This is a great mode for use over the minor seventh tonic chord C Eb G Bb. As is the case with all of the other Bebop scales, other chromatic notes can be brought into play under the cover of the Bebop Dorian scale.

The Jazz Minor Scale

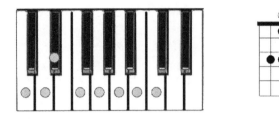

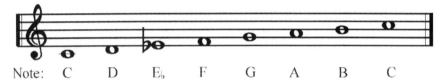

Note: C   D   E♭   F   G   A   B   C

Scale Origin: Classical.

Scale Type: Heptatonic.

Tuning: Twelve-tone equal temperament.

Styles of Music: Various.

Transposition: 2 – 1 – 2 – 2 – 2 -2 – 1.

Features: Traditional forms of minor scale are popular in jazz. The natural minor scale has already been covered in the section that deals with diatonic scale. Jazz also uses the harmonic and melodic forms of minor scale. However, the melodic minor scale mostly tends to be used in its ascending form. Indeed, it is used so often that it has now acquired the name of the Jazz minor scale.

Also popular in jazz is the use of the various modes of the harmonic and melodic minor scale. These are obtained by choosing a degree of the scale other than the customary first degree, as the starting point of the scale. As far as the harmonic minor mode is concerned therefore, there are seven such sub-modes, while there are also seven sub-modes of the melodic minor.

The ascending form of the melodic minor scale is created by sharpening the sixth and seventh of the natural minor scale. In classical styles of music, these alterations were cancelled upon descent in order to create a smooth melodic descent to the fifth degree of the scale. In the context of jazz, only the rising form of the melodic minor scale is relevant. Jazz has made this scale its own due to its particular use of the scale – which again bears very little relationship to classical music. For this reason, this scale is often simply referred to as the jazz minor scale.

Jazz Harmonic Minor Scale

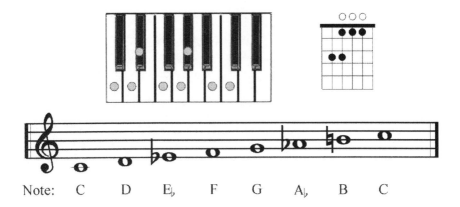

| Note: | C | D | E♭ | F | G | A♭ | B | C |

Scale Origin: Western classical music.

Scale Type: Heptatonic.

Tuning: Twelve-tone equal temperament.

Styles of Music: Various.

Transposition: 2 – 1 – 2 – 2 – 1 – 3 – 1.

Features: The harmonic minor scale is a modal variant of the natural minor scale (Aeolian mode) obtained by sharpening the seventh degree. This scale will often be heard being used in Latin American jazz. Various modes of this scale are also popular in Klezmer styles. Although originally 'borrowed' from classical music, the use of this scale in jazz is quite distinct from that earlier tradition. This is for two main reasons.

The first is that in jazz, each degree of the scale is considered to provide the root note, not for a triad – major, minor, augmented or diminished – but a seventh chord. In classical music, the chord of the seventh was considered dissonant and there were particular rules developed for the treatment of the dissonant notes contained in these chords. In jazz however, this dissonance is an integral feature of the style, which means it is treated as an essential part of each chord. Consequently, there is no felt need for the seventh or any other chordal extension, to resolve to a consonance. This practice produces that characteristic rich chordal texture which we associate with jazz generally.

The Augmented Scale

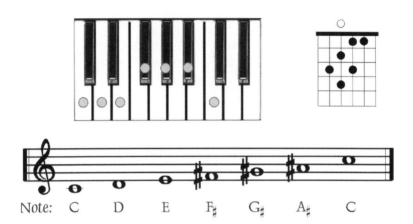

Note: C   D   E   F♯   G♯   A♯   C

Scale Origin: Russian classical music.

Scale Type: Hexatonic.

Tuning: Twelve-tone equal temperament.

Styles of Music: Jazz.

Transposition: 2 – 2 – 2 – 2 – 2 – 2.

Features: Jazz scales that use regular interval cycles are called symmetrical scales. These play an important part in the modern language of jazz, both in terms of the use of such scales for the purposes of improvisation and in terms of the creation of chord progressions, which may provide an important underlying framework for improvisation.

In terms of the latter, these are created by taking each note of an interval cycle as a prospective chordal root. This applies to the use of both simple cycles composed of only one uniform interval, and compound cycles composed of numerous intervals. As the study of these falls under the general jurisdiction of jazz harmony, here we will primarily focus upon the use of symmetric scales in the process of improvisation.

The unit of measurement of those interval cycles that generate symmetric scales is the semitone. If a unit of one semitone is used as the generator, then a cycle of twelve stages, which progressively moves through all of the semitones of the chromatic scale, will be obtained. In effect therefore, the chromatic scale is itself an example of a *symmetric scale*. Moreover, as far as the melodic and harmonic language of jazz is built upon the foundation of the chromatic scale, this means that the basic scale of jazz is itself a symmetrical scale of twelve-notes.

Symmetric scales other than the chromatic can be obtained by generating various interval cycles using units composed of a certain number of semitones. The two main scales belonging to this category are the augmented scale and the diminished scale.

If an interval of two-semitones, i.e. a whole tone, is taken as the generating interval, a symmetric scale of six whole tones in the octave is created. Jazz musicians call this the augmented scale. Consisting of six successive whole tones it is often referred to in other styles of music as the whole tone scale – a scale that has a strong association with modern classical music. In jazz, the whole tone scale plays an important role as a scalar expression of various chromatically altered dominant harmonies. These are important in jazz as they offer to chords of dominant colours a number of distinctive chromatic shades.

The Diminished Scale

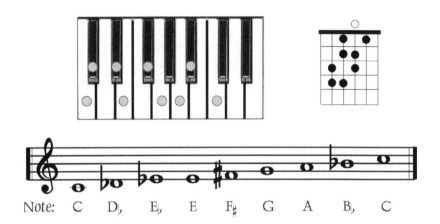

Note: C D♭ E♭ E F♯ G A B♭ C

Scale Origin: Russian classical music.

Scale Type: Octatonic.

Tuning: Twelve-tone equal temperament.

Styles of Music: Jazz.

Transposition: 1 – 2 – 1 – 2 – 1 – 2 -1 - 2.

Features: A cycle that uses an interval of three semitones – a minor third - as the generator produces a cycle of four notes which, as a group, form a diminished seventh chord - the seventh chord obtained on the seventh degree of the harmonic minor scale. The diminished scale is a scale of alternating tones and semitones built around this chord.

In jazz, the diminished scale therefore finds its principle use as a scale for improvisation over chords of the diminished seventh, dominant seventh and chords of the dominant flat ninth. When used with a diminished seventh chord the scale tends to begin on the root of the diminished seventh chord.

Section 7: Pentatonic Scales of Japanese Music

Musicians of the West tend to take a great interest in the musical languages of other cultures. Naturally, one area in which this interest shows itself is in terms of the particular musical scales used by a given musical culture. Some of these scales are quite unlike any musical scales found in the West. The scales of Indonesian gamelan music, characterized by a particular and unique method of tuning, fall into this category. Other scales are somehow familiar, and can often be found in a variety of forms which Western musicians have been quick to adapt and use.

In this latter category belong numerous scales which originate from traditional Japanese traditional music. Embracing the repertoire of instruments such as the koto, shamisen and shakuhachi flute, most of the scales used are purely pentatonic, some of which have a perceptible Chinese influence. Others are uniquely Japanese, and possess certain characteristics which give melodies written in those scales, a peculiar charm and expressive power, which has always commended them to musicians.

One of the salient features of these is the use of major third pentatonics, that is pentatonic scales which divide the fourth into a major third and semitone, as opposed to the more regular minor third pentatonics which divide the fourth into a minor third and whole tone. The latter, although used in Japanese traditional music, tend to have a strong association with Chinese traditional music.

In this section we will consider some of the main pentatonic scales that, having originally been used in Japanese traditional music, were then later borrowed and used by musicians in the West.

Ryo

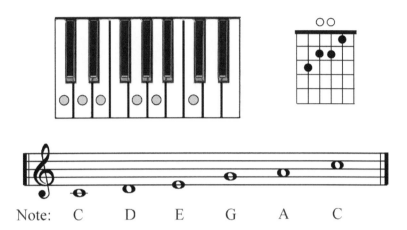

Note: C   D   E   G   A   C

Origin: Chinese/Japanese.

Scale Type: Anhemitonic pentatonic.

Tuning: In perfect fifths/fourths.

Styles of Music: Japanese traditional.

Transposition: 2 – 2 – 3 – 2 – 3.

Features: While Japanese musicians were fully aware of the five pentatonic modes of Chinese music, only two or three of these tended to be used in practice.

The most important of these were Ryo, corresponding to the Chinese Gong mode, equivalent to the Western major pentatonic scale, and Ritsu corresponding to the Chinese Zhi mode, equivalent to the Western suspended pentatonic scale.

Ryo and Ritsu are the basic scales of shōmyō, a style of Buddhist chant originally imported from China by way of Korea. In contrast to Ritsu, which was considered to be yang or masculine in its nature, Ryo modes were considered to be yin or female in nature.

Ritsu

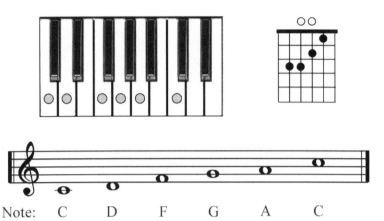

Note: C   D   F   G   A   C

Origin: Chinese/Japanese.

Scale Type: Anhemitonic pentatonic.

Tuning: In perfect fifths/fourths.

Styles of Music: Japanese traditional.

Transposition: 2 – 3 – 2 – 2 – 3.

Features: Ritsu is the counterpart pentatonic scale to Ryo. The difference lies in the placement of kaku, the third degree of the scale. In Ritsu kaku is a semitone higher. Ritsu modes are traditionally considered to be yang, sunny or male in their nature.

Minyō

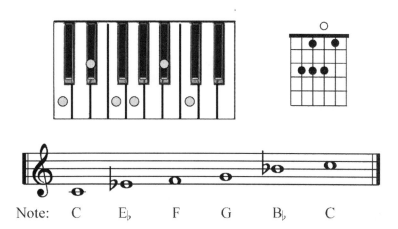

Note: C   E♭   F   G   B♭   C

Origin: Chinese/Japanese.

Scale Type: Anhemitonic pentatonic.

Tuning: In perfect fifths/fourths.

Transposition: 3 – 2 – 2 – 3 – 2.

Styles of Music: Shakuhachi.

Features: Minyō is an important pentatonic scale in the shakuhachi flute repertoire. The shakuhachi has a beautiful, mellow haunting sound and was commonly played by Zen Buddhist monks as a form of mediation. The shakuhachi flute is tuned by default to this scale. Minyō is generally considered to be a folk music scale, and corresponds to the minor pentatonic scale of Western music.

Hirajoshi

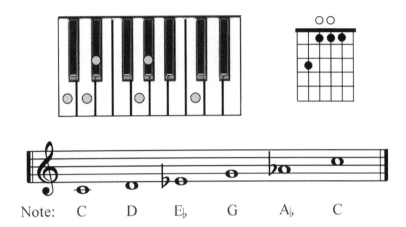

Note:　C　　　D　　　E♭　　　G　　　A♭　　　C

Origin:　　　　　Japanese.

Scale Type:　　　Hemitonic pentatonic.

Tuning:　　　　In perfect fifths/fourths.

Styles of Music:　Koto.

Transposition:　2 – 1 – 4 – 1 – 4.

Features: Hirajoshi is a quintessentially Japanese pentatonic scale, quite distinct from Chinese pentatonic scales owing to the characteristic use of major third pentatonics. Major third pentatonic scales use semitones, which in the case of Hirajoshi, lie between the second and third and fourth and fifth degrees of the pentatonic scale.

Pentatonic scales that use semitones are called hemitonic as opposed to the more typical anhemitonic pentatonic scale of China, associated with minor third pentatonic scales.

Kumoi Joshi

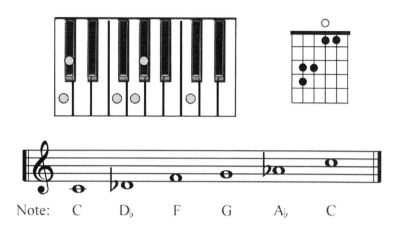

Note: C   D♭   F   G   A♭   C

Origin: Japanese.

Scale Type: Hemitonic pentatonic.

Tuning: In perfect fifths/fourths.

Styles of Music: Koto.

Transposition: 1 – 4 – 2 – 1 – 4.

Features: Kumoi Joshi is another hemitonic pentatonic scale derived originally from a koto tuning. Like Hirajoshi, Kumoi Joshi is a major third pentatonic scale. In effect this means that it uses semitones between adjacent scale degrees. The difference between the two lies in their positions relative to the scale as a whole. In Kumoi Joshi the semitones are between the first and second, and the fourth and fifth degrees of the pentatonic scale. The well known Japanese air Sakura, Sakura is written in this mode.

Iwato

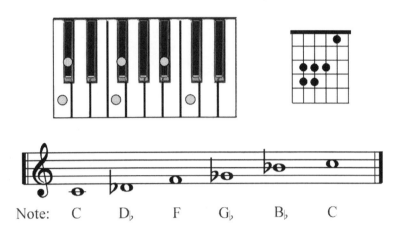

Note:　C　　D♭　　F　　G♭　　B♭　　C

Origin:　　　　　Japanese.

Scale Type:　　　Hemitonic pentatonic.

Tuning:　　　　In perfect fifths/fourths.

Styles of Music:　Koto.

Transposition:　　1 – 4 – 1 – 4 – 2.

Features: Iwato is another pentatonic mode derived from an original koto tuning. It belongs to the hemitonic pentatonic scales group, using as it does semitones s pentatonic scale steps. These lie between the first and second and third and fourth degrees of the pentatonic scale. Hirajoshi, Kumoi Joshi and Iwato are all modes of the same basic pentatonic scale.

Kokin Joshi

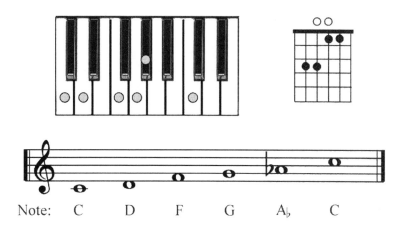

Note: C   D   F   G   A♭   C

Origin: Japanese.

Scale Type: Hemitonic pentatonic.

Tuning: In perfect fifths/fourths.

Styles of Music: Koto.

Transposition: 2 – 3 – 2 – 1 – 4.

Features: Kokin Joshi is another Japanese pentatonic scale derived from a koto tuning. It's make-up is interesting, consisting as it does of a fascinating blend of major and minor third pentatonics. The lower trichord between the notes C and F is anhemitonic, consisting of a tone and a minor third, while the upper trichord is hemitonic, consisting of a minor second and a major third.

Akebono

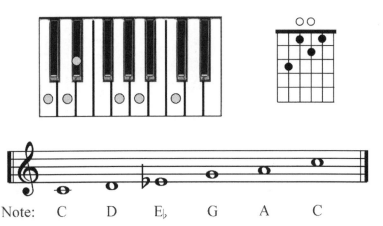

Note: C   D   E♭   G   A   C

Origin: Japanese.

Scale Type: Hemitonic pentatonic.

Tuning: In perfect fifths/fourths.

Styles of Music: Koto.

Transposition: 2 – 1 – 4 – 2 – 3.

Features: Like Kokin Joshi, Akebono is a mixture of major and minor third pentatonics. Therefore the lower half of the scale is hemitonic, while the upper half is anhemitonic. Akebono is the third mode of Kokin Joshi.

Han Iwato

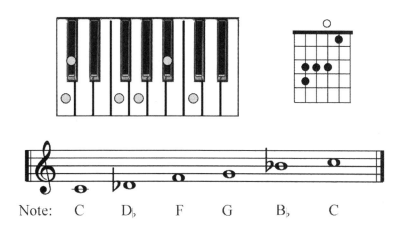

Note: C   D♭   F   G   B♭   C

Origin: Japanese

Scale Type: Hemitonic pentatonic.

Tuning: In perfect fifths/fourths.

Styles of Music: Koto

Transposition: 1 – 4 – 2 – 3 – 2.

Features: Han Iwato is another pentatonic scale derived from a koto tuning. The lower trichord is hemitonic, consisting of a minor second and a major third while the upper trichord is anhemitonic consisting of a minor third and a whole tone. Kokin Joshi, Akebono and Han Iwato are all modes of the same basic pentatonic scale.

Ryukuan

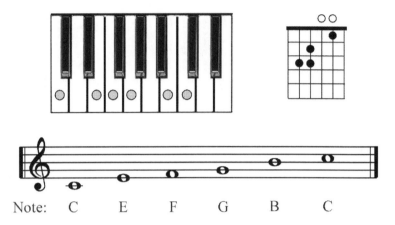

Note: C   E   F   G   B   C

Origin: Japanese.

Scale Type: Hemitonic pentatonic.

Tuning: In perfect fifths/fourths.

Styles of Music: Okinawan folk music.

Transposition: 4 – 1 – 2 – 4 – 1.

Features: Ryukuan is a pentatonic scale associated with the folk music of the Okinawan prefecture of Japan. It belongs to the hemitonic group of pentatonic modes although its intervals are arranged with respect to a major type scale, the second and sixth of which are characteristically absent. This gives it an absolutely unique sound found nowhere else in the world except perhaps, for certain parts of Ethiopia, whose native musicians sometimes use a similar mode.

Yosenpo

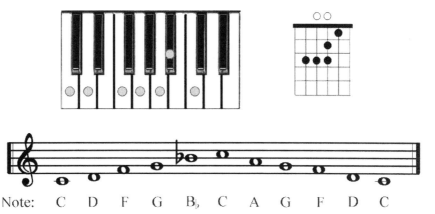

Note: C   D   F   G   B♭   C   A   G   F   D   C

Origin: Japanese.

Scale Type: Pentatonic/hexatonic.

Tuning: In perfect fifths/fourths.

Styles of Music: Japanese traditional.

Features: One of the most popular and enduring theories of the Japanese scale system is that are just two basic scales of Japanese traditional music. There is the Yosenpo scale – referred to as Yo for short – and the Insenpo scale. The Yosenpo scale, shown here, uses regular minor third pentatonics and is generally associated with folk music. Note that like the Western melodic minor scale, the rising form is different to the falling form. The Japanese national anthem is based on the Yosenpo scale.

Insenpo

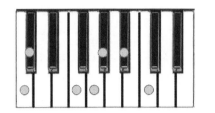

Note: C   D♭   F   G   B♭   C   A♭   G   F   D♭   C

Origin: Japanese.

Scale Type: Pentatonic/hexatonic.

Tuning: In perfect fifths/fourths.

Styles of Music: Japanese traditional.

Features: In contrast to the Yosenpo scale which uses minor third pentatonics, there is the Insenpo scale, shown here which uses major third pentatonics. While the former is associated with folk music, the latter is associated with the more refined classical repertoire of instruments such as the koto and shamisen.

Section 8: Ethiopian Kiñit

Excepting perhaps for the maqam scales used in the Maghreb area of North Africa, the traditional and popular music of Ethiopia uses one of the most highly developed modal systems used throughout this region of the world.

In general, traditional Ethiopian music uses a wide variety of musical scales. These can have any number of notes from a few, often used in folk and children songs, up to the full complement of seven. The latter are used particularly in *zema*, the chant tradition of the Ethiopian Orthodox Christian Church, the foundations for which were laid down by Jared, a sixth century holy musician. On the secular front, Ethiopia is famous for its *amzaris*, wandering troubadours who traditionally provided music for every possible occasion.

Ethiopian traditional music has a beautiful, unique and distinctive sound, due in part to the skilful use of traditional instruments such as the *krar* - a six-stringed lyre, the *begenta* – a ten-stringed lyre and the *masenka* – a single stringed lute. Much of the beauty and great expressive power of Ethiopian music however, is due to the use of a distinctive and unique modal system that is called *kiñit*.

One of the curious features of *kiñit* is that, like much of the music of the Far East, the main focus of the modal system is the pentatonic scale of five notes. Although this naturally prompts a comparison with Far Eastern musical cultures, Ethiopian music has its own unique approach to music making which makes all such comparisons superficial.

One of the clearest and most useful recent expositions of *kiñit* was made by Ezra Abate of the Jared Musical School, who spoke and wrote extensively on the subject in the 16th International Conference of Ethiopian Studies (2009). Thanks to Abate's clear explanations, the whole subject of *kiñit* has now become much more accessible to the ordinary musician. Indeed, it is due to scholars such as Abate, that the scales belonging to the Ethiopian *kiñit* system are now attracting increasing attention from musicians worldwide.

The fascination with *kiñit* lies in the wide variety of pentatonic modes that are used, which occur both in anhemitonic and hemitonic forms. Among these we find some of the most beautiful and distinctive pentatonic modes of world music. These in their turn, underlie a rich and varied repertoire of songs whose distinctive beauty and power of expression captures everybody who cares to listen to them.

The modes belonging to the *kiñit* system generally break down into four main branches or modal types, which are *Tizita, Batti, Ambassel* and *Anchihoye*. There are also a number of other pentatonic modes, which tend to float about between categories. Each of these modes is associated with certain traditional songs that use them and best convey their particular characteristics. The feeling, mood or spirit of these songs then becomes linked and associated with the modes themselves. In this way, each mode then becomes charged with certain emotive associations which, like the maqam scales of Middle Eastern music, or Hindustani raga, then act as a guide and signpost towards a proper interpretation and musical mode of expression.

Tizita Major

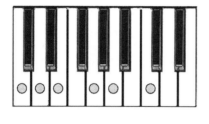

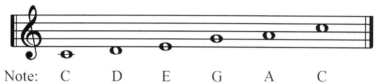

Note: C   D   E   G   A   C

Origin: Ethiopia.

Scale Type: Anhemitonic pentatonic.

Tuning: Varies.

Styles of Music: Ethiopian traditional and popular music.

Transposition: 2 – 2 – 3 – 2 – 3.

Features: Tizita is the first of four families of modes belonging to the Ethiopian pentatonic modal system kiñit. The names of the four families stem from the names of traditional songs in which these modes tend to be used. Consequently, there is a direct perceived link between the feeling of the song and the modes themselves.

There are two main modes belonging to this family, which are Tizita major and Tizita minor. Tizita major, shown here, is identical with the major pentatonic scale of Western music. Its modal colour tones, the major second, third and sixth give it a bright quality.

169

Tizita Minor

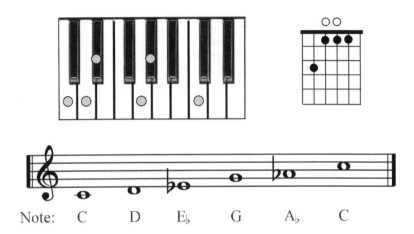

Note: C   D   E♭   G   A♭   C

Origin: Ethiopia.

Scale Type: Hemitonic pentatonic.

Tuning: Varies.

Styles of Music: Ethiopian traditional and popular music.

Transposition: 2 – 1 – 4 – 1 – 4.

Features: To produce the Tizita minor mode, the third and sixth of Tizita major are flattened by a semitone. This produces a hemitonic pentatonic mode very similar to some of the modal forms of traditional Japanese music. However, because of the way in which this mode is used in traditional songs, it undoubtedly has a distinctly Ethiopian sound. The minor third and sixth are the main modal colour tones, which give to this mode its darker, sadder quality.

Batti Major

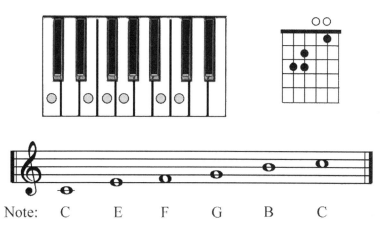

Note: C   E   F   G   B   C

Origin: Ethiopia.

Scale Type: Hemitonic pentatonic.

Tuning: Varies.

Styles of Music: Ethiopian traditional and popular music.

Transposition: 4 – 1 – 2 – 4 – 1.

Features: Batti is the second family of pentatonic modes belonging to the modal system of kiñit. Batti is a hemitonic pentatonic scale, which means to say that it makes use of major third pentatonics. These major thirds can be found between the notes C and E and G and B. This gives rise to a mode that is very similar to the Western major scale with second and sixth omitted. The main modal colour tones are the major third and seventh which give this a mode a bright, hard and glittering quality.

Batti Major #4

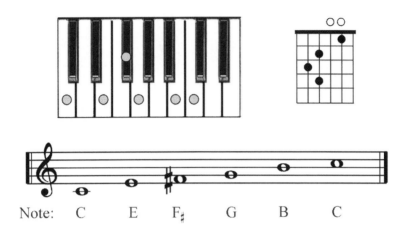

Note: C   E   F♯   G   B   C

Origin: Ethiopia.

Scale Type: Hemitonic pentatonic.

Tuning: Varies.

Styles of Music: Ethiopian traditional and popular music.

Transposition: 4 – 2 – 1 – 4 – 1.

Features: Ethiopian musicians use several common variations of the Batti major mode. One such variation sharpens the fourth to produce a Lydian type pentatonic mode, shown above. Coupled with the major third and seventh – the two other modal colour tones, Batti major has a bright, mystical quality.

Batti Major #5

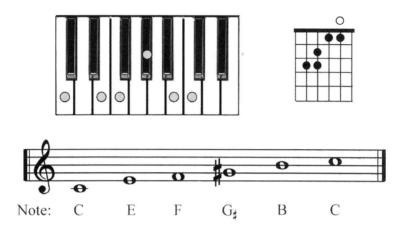

Note: C   E   F   G♯   B   C

Origin: Ethiopia.

Scale Type: Hemitonic pentatonic.

Tuning: Varies.

Styles of Music: Ethiopian traditional and popular music.

Transposition: 4 – 1 – 3 – 3 – 1.

Features: Another variation of Batti major is obtained by sharpening the fifth. This produces a distinctive pentatonic mode which, coincidentally, is also used in Romanian music, where it is called Bacovia.

Batti Minor

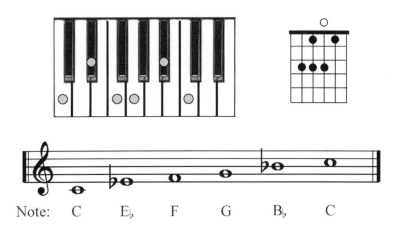

Note: C   E♭   F   G   B♭   C

Origin: Ethiopia.

Scale Type: Anhemitonic pentatonic.

Tuning: Varies.

Styles of Music: Ethiopian traditional and popular music.

Transposition: 3 – 2 – 2 – 3 – 2.

Features: Batti minor can be derived from Batti major by flattening the third and seventh. This produces a form of pentatonic scale that Western musicians know as the minor pentatonic – a very useful and versatile scale that finds an application in a great variety of different styles of music. The main modal colour tones are the minor third and seventh which give to this mode its mellow colour.

Batti Minor 4#

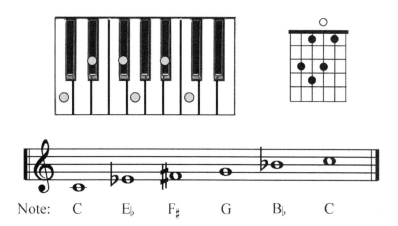

Note: C   E♭   F♯   G   B♭   C

Origin: Ethiopia.

Scale Type: Hemitonic pentatonic.

Tuning: Varies.

Styles of Music: Ethiopian traditional and popular music.

Transposition: 3 – 3 – 1 – 3 – 2.

Features: Ethiopian musicians use a number of variants of Batti minor. One such variant is obtained by sharpening the fourth. This produces a scale that to Western musicians at least, has a distinctive blues sound.

Batti Minor 4/7#

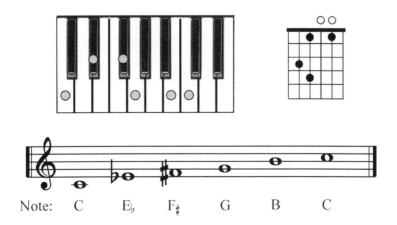

Note: C   E♭   F♯   G   B   C

Origin: Ethiopia.

Scale Type: Hemitonic pentatonic.

Tuning: Varies.

Styles of Music: Ethiopian traditional and popular music.

Transposition: 3 – 3 – 1 – 4 – 1.

Features: Another variant of Batti minor is obtained by flattening only the third of Batti major. This produces a scale very similar to the Hungarian minor mode – except that in this case the second and sixth are characteristically absent.

Ambassel (Major)

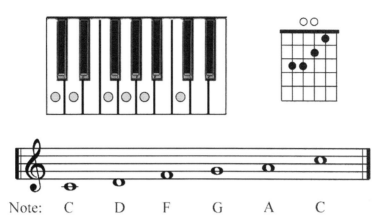

Note: C   D   F   G   A   C

Origin: Ethiopia.

Scale Type: Anhemitonic pentatonic.

Tuning: Varies.

Styles of Music: Ethiopian traditional and popular music.

Transposition: 2 – 3 – 2 – 2 – 3.

Features: The third family of kiñit modes is Ambassel, of which Ambassel major as shown above, is the basic form. Ambassel major is a regular form of pentatonic scale consisting of two trichords separated by a whole tone. Each trichord is divisible into a whole tone and a minor third. The main modal colour tones are the major second and sixth.

Ambassel (Minor)

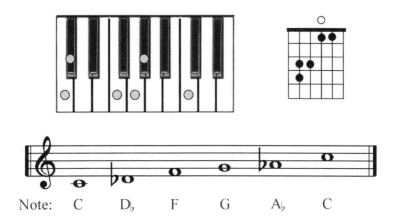

| Note: | C | D♭ | F | G | A♭ | C |

Origin: Ethiopia.

Scale Type: Hemitonic pentatonic.

Tuning: Varies.

Styles of Music: Ethiopian traditional and popular music.

Transposition: 1 – 4 – 2 – 1 – 4.

Features: Ambassel minor is obtained by flattening the second and sixth of Ambassel major. This produces a pentatonic scale that in Japanese music is known as kumoi joshi. However the sound of Ambassel minor is very distinctive, as can be heard by listening to Ambassel being sung by a well known Ethiopian artist such as Mahmoud Ahmed (b. 1941).

Ambassel minor is again divisible into two trichords, although in this case the trichords are divided into a semitone and a major third. As such, Ambassel major and minor bear a similar relationship to one another as the Yo and In scales of Japanese music. The main modal colour tones are the minor second and sixth.

Anchihoye

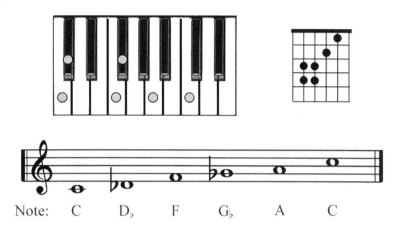

Note: C   D♭   F   G♭   A   C

Origin: Ethiopia.

Scale Type: Hemitonic pentatonic.

Tuning: Varies.

Styles of Music: Ethiopian traditional and popular music.

Transposition: 1 – 4 – 1 – 3 – 3.

Features: The fourth group of modes in the kiñit system is Anchihoye. Like the other groups of modes, Anchihoye is named after a popular song of that name, *Anchihoye Lene*. The unique feature of Anchihoye is its diminished fifth, a modal colour tone that gives to Anchihoye much of its distinctive and unique sound.

Yematebela Wofe

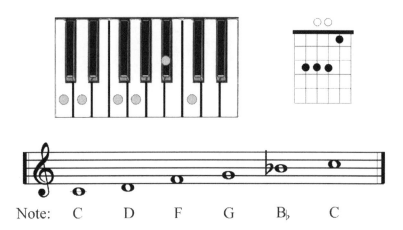

Note: C   D   F   G   B♭   C

Origin: Ethiopia.

Scale Type: Anhemitonic pentatonic.

Tuning: Varies.

Styles of Music: Ethiopian traditional and popular music.

Transposition: 2 – 3 – 2 – 3 – 2.

Features: Yematebela Wofe is one of the regular anhemitonic forms of pentatonic scale used in Ethiopian music. It is named after a song that uses this mode prominently. Yematebela Wofe is the third mode of the regular form of pentatonic scale, of which Tizita is the first.

Shegaye

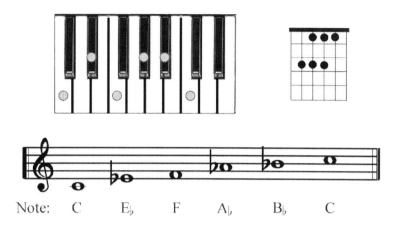

Note: C   E♭   F   A♭   B♭   C

Origin: Ethiopia.

Scale Type: Anhemitonic pentatonic.

Tuning: Varies.

Styles of Music: Ethiopian traditional and popular music.

Transposition: 3 – 2 – 3 – 2 – 2.

Features: Another of the regular minor third pentatonic scales used in Ethiopian traditional music is Shegaye, which is the fifth mode of the regular pentatonic scale.

Section 9: Indonesian Scales of the Gamelan

While Western musicians are usually content to play, produce and compose music using the twelve-tone chromatic scale to which instruments such as the keyboard, organ, piano and guitar are tuned, they often forget that in other parts of the world, not only are different musical scales used, but in many cases, they are tuned using different methods of tuning.

Examples of this are the just intonation scales of the Indian subcontinent in which the intervals of the scale are tuned according to pure harmonic ratios, examples of which are 2/1, the ratio of the octave, 3/2 the ratio of the perfect fifth and 5/4 the ratio of the major third. Another example are the pentatonic scales of China and Japan which were originally tuned using pure fifths and fourths of ratio 3/2 and 4/3 respectively.

In our Western twelve-tone scale these pure intervals are compromised by distributing their differences in such a way as to create a scale of twelve mathematically equal semitones. This type of tuning is called equal temperament. The result is a scale of great facility, but one in which the acoustic purity of the intervals is compromised. In fact the only pure interval used in the equally tempered twelve tone scale is the octave of ratio 2/1.

In the next section we are going to introduce a number of scales that do use different types of tuning to the West. In many cases, the particular tuning can easily be realized on modern synthesizers, in either hardware or software forms. For those who wish to experiment with this, this is a very fruitful area, and can lead to the creation of a unique or distinctive sound.

Those who are familiar with the just intonation experiments of Wendy Carlos (b. 1939) will no doubt be aware of this. Carlos has designed numerous unique scales using the principles of just intonation which she uses in particular compositions, a good example of which is *Beauty in the Beast* (1986).

In certain cases musicians often borrow scales which although designed with a different tuning in mind, adapt well when brought over into twelve-tone equal temperament. A good example of this are the various mela of Carnatic music which will be introduced in the appropriate section.

In other cases, such as the scales used in Indonesian Gamelan music, Thai ensemble music or African kora music, the tuning is more or less an indispensible feature of the sound. Consequently to try and bring these scales over and adapt them to the Western scale is often to lose a great part of their original charm.

In this case therefore, experiments are best conducted on instruments such as modern synthesizers, which enable the tuning of individual notes to be adjusted. These adjustments are generally made by way of cents, each cent being equivalent to 1/100th of an equally tempered semitone.

For those instruments that do enable adjustments of tuning in cents, the cents values for each note of the following scales will be given. These will enable the musician to accurately tune their instrument to those scales. The result will be a specially tuned scale with which to undertake a fascinating personal exploration of the musical treasures of another, often far distant land. We will begin this by considering the scales used in Indonesian Gamelan orchestras.

Some of the most individual and unique musical scales that have ever been developed originate from the Indonesian archipelago. To be able to appreciate these scales, it would perhaps be expedient at this stage, to go into a brief discussion of the music of this particular area.

Because of the unique geography of this region, the music of Indonesia is not only very diverse, but also noted for the great individuality of local styles and cultural traditions. Yet running across this, is a certain homogeneity of sound due to the ease of accessibility of particular materials used for the construction of traditional musical instruments. This includes wood and bamboo obtained from the tropical rain forests and in particular bronze, the techniques for casting of which, were brought over from the mainland a couple of thousand years ago.

Instruments made from bamboo include flutes, tube zithers, lutes, and xylophones, the latter also being made using tuned slabs of wood. The popularity of bronze gongs, bells, and chimes is particularly notable, and it is largely the widespread use of such instruments that tends give much of Indonesian traditional music its characteristic sound. The use of entire orchestras of such instruments – called *gamelans* - is a notable trait, particularly on the isles of Java and Bali.

The prevalent use of tuned percussion instruments helps to give the music of this region of the world much of its unique texture and characteristic spectrum of tone colours – a spectrum that Western listeners find particularly fascinating – especially when compared with Western orchestras. The quote given offers some sense of this fascination: "GAMELAN is comparable only to two things: moonlight and flowing water. It is pure and mysterious like moonlight; it is always the same and always changing like flowing water. "

The above words convey the impression the music of the *gamelan* made upon the Dutch writer Leonhard Huizinga (1906 – 1980) in his encounters with the music of Indonesia in the 1930's. The metaphors he uses of moonlight and flowing water vividly relate a sense of the beautiful shimmering tone colours produced by the gamelan orchestra. These colours are largely due to the predominance of instruments of metallic timbres, such as knobbed and hanging gongs of different sizes, metallophones made from tuned metal bars and rows of tuned gong chimes of different sizes. These, together with instruments such as two-stringed fiddles imported from the Middle East (rebab), bamboo flutes, zithers and various types of percussion instruments make up the distinctive ensemble that is the Indonesian gamelan orchestra.

Learning to appreciate the music of the gamelan can often take some time. This is because of the way the music tends to be organized. There is very little sense of the vertical element of harmony, the music instead tending to focus more on the horizontal element. Here, numerous lines or melodic parts may be heard intertwining, often seeming to clash in ways that display a linear, rather than harmonic approach to composition. This technique is known as *heterophony* and counts as one of the most common methods of musical organization used in traditional Southeast Asian music.

To learn to appreciate this heterophonic style it is probably best to learn to listen to this music in a different way. This entails listening to the music on its own terms. Rather than listening out for thematic development or chord progressions, instead it is probably best to let go and surrender to the often-sensual interplay of shimmering tone colours, without any sense or expectancy that the music should be *going somewhere*.

The heterophonic organization of gamelan music particularly impressed the composer Claude Debussy. Indeed, he wrote, "Javanese music obeys laws of counterpoint which make Palestrina seem like child's play. And if one listens to it without being prejudiced by one's European ears, one will find a percussive charm that forces one to admit that our own music is not much more than a barbarous kind of noise fit for a travelling circus"[28]

The charm that Debussy speaks of is due to numerous factors. One of these is the way in which the music is meticulously organized. The different horizontal layers of the music are coordinated temporally through reference to a framework of periodic cycles that form the essential backdrop to the music. These cycles are called gongan, a typical cycle consisting of eight or sixteen pulses.

A large gong announces the beginning of the cycle, while a progressively smaller series of gongs announce the various halves, quarters and eighths of the cycle. These form the backdrop for the main melody, called the balungan in Java or the pokok in Bali. Played on large keyed metallophones, the main melody is then used as a subject for elaboration by the other instruments of the orchestra.

---

[28] Richard Langham Smith, *Debussy on Music*, p. 138.

The charm of the sound of the gamelan is also due to the use of certain unique types of musical scales. When these scales are studied, it soon becomes apparent that our Western conceptions of musical scales have very little bearing. Indeed, a mostly pentatonic tonal world presents itself, very reminiscent of the scales used in traditional Chinese, Japanese, Tibetan and Korean music, except that in Indonesia, these scales have been subtly transformed, modified, and given an altogether new identity.

One such feature of this is the Balinese practice of tuning pairs of instruments slightly differently so that when played simultaneously, they create a beautiful shimmering effect. Although this adjustment amounts to a tiny increment, the effect it has on the resultant sound is noticeably significant.

An important feature of gamelan scales is a much more flexible approach to the spaces between the notes. These spaces are not fixed or regulated by mathematical considerations of pipe or string length. Instead, the ear tends to be the sole arbiter of what is acceptable or not. This leads to the creation of scales, which, although strangely familiar due to their archaic origins, are nonetheless touched by a sense of the unknown and the unfamiliar.

Slendro

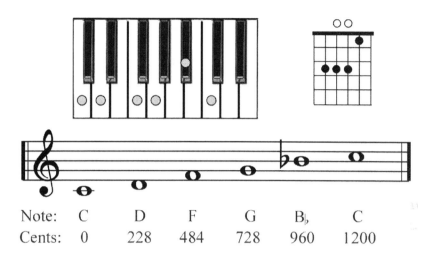

Note:	C	D	F	G	B♭	C
Cents:	0	228	484	728	960	1200

Origin: Indonesia.

Scale Type: Pentatonic.

Tuning: Five *approximately* equal intervals.

Styles of Music: Gamelan music.

Transposition: 2 – 3 – 2 – 3 – 2.

Features: Gamelan orchestras are tuned to two main scales: *slendro and pelog*. Both scales are characterized by a unique tuning method, which helps to distinguish one from the other. For this reason, tuned gamelan instruments are often paired in order to provide for the playing of music in either tuning as the case may be.

Slendro is a five-toned or pentatonic scale used by both Javanese and Balinese gamelans. It is also used by the Kulintang ensembles of east Malaysia.

The notes as portrayed on both the keyboard and the guitar fret board are simply the nearest approximate equivalents to the notes of the *slendro* scale in Western notation. Equivalents are given because except for the first degree of the scale, all of the notes of *slendro* fall 'between the cracks' of the keyboard.

The degree of divergence from Western tempered intervals can be gauged by looking at the cents measurements for each note of the scale. The second note *dong* is 28 cents larger than a major tone, the third note *deng*, 16 cents smaller than a tempered fourth; *dung* is 28 cents larger than a tempered fifth, while *dang* is 40 cents smaller than a tempered minor seventh. The cents measurements are those given by Alexander Ellis (1814 – 1890) in his paper *On the Musical Scales of Various Nations* (1885).

In similarity with other cultures that use pentatonic scales, the five notes of slendro are symbolically linked with the five directions: North, South, East, West and Centre.[29] Of the five, the centre is generally considered most important. Indeed, throughout the various mythologies of the world, the directional centre is often taken to be symbolic of the source of a sacred creative power that, radiating out from the centre, was considered to continually refresh and rejuvenate the world. This process of radiation has often been envisioned as flowing from the centre outwards towards all four directions of manifestation. The flow of this creative power has therefore been variously symbolized in terms of directions, divinities, winds, elements, rivers, pillars or supports upon which the maintenance of the world and its well-being was seen to depend.

In the more localized context of Balinese music, the centre signifies the Hindu God Shiva, a divinity who in the context of this cosmological scheme, McPhee describes as "Creator, Destroyer, and lord God of All".[30] Often visualized sitting at the centre of a lotus, the petals radiating out from the centre thereby correspond to the other tones of the scale. These are accordingly consecrated to the Gods of the cardinal

---

[29] Colin McPhee, *Music in Bali: A Study in Form and Instrumental Organization in Balinese Orchestral Music*, p. 38.
[30] Colin McPhee, *A House in Bali*, p. 43.

directions. In this context, gamelan music aims to connect with that higher, sacred source. Gamelan music thus has powerful spiritual sympathies with the music of China, Tibet and Korea - where the pentatonic scale is also prevalent.

However, although resembling early Chinese prototypes of the pentatonic scale, the *Slendro* scale has evolved its own unique tuning which makes it one of the most distinctive and colorful scales used in world music, especially suited to the metallic timbres of the instruments of the Gamelan orchestra.

The uniqueness of *slendro* tuning lies in the increase of the size of the tones and the decrease in the size of the minor thirds of the pentatonic scale to result in an approximately equal five-toned division of the octave. This means that theoretically at least, each scale step in *slendro* would measure 240 cents. However, composer and acknowledged Western authority on gamelan music Colin McPhee (1900 – 1964) observed that while 240 cents represented an ideal, that in practice the scale steps were tuned to provide a contrast between larger and smaller intervals.[31]

Yet even the degree of difference between such larger and smaller intervals is virtually impossible to quantify in any general sense. Every gamelan orchestra tends to be tuned differently. Therefore, while an orchestra in one village might use one tuning, in the next village the instruments are tuned differently. Consequently, no two tunings tend to be exactly alike. Ethnomusicologist Jaap Kunst (1891 – 1960) illustrates this important point in his book *Music in Java (1949)*, where in *Appendix 62* he presents no less than 46 different tunings for the *Slendro* scale.

---

[31] Colin McPhee, *Music in Bali: A Study in Form and Instrumental Organization in Balinese Orchestral Music*, p. 50.

This variation of tuning no doubt contributes to the individual sound of each gamelan orchestra, a sound which Wayne Vitale ingeniously compared to a "vineyard-designated vintage wine" [32]

---

[32] Wayne Vitale, *Balinese Kebyar Music Breaks the Five Tone Barrier: New Composition for Seven-Tone Gamelan*, p. 10.

Pelog

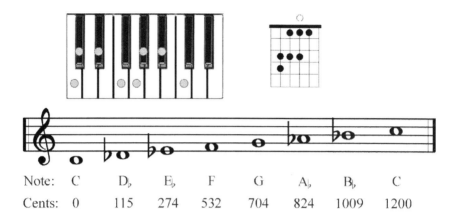

Note:	C	D♭	E♭	F	G	A♭	B♭	C
Cents:	0	115	274	532	704	824	1009	1200

Origin: Indonesia.

Scale Type: Pentatonic with two auxiliaries.

Tuning: By ear.

Styles of Music: Gamelan music.

Transposition: 1 – 2 – 2 – 2 – 1 – 2 – 2.

Features: Pelog is the second main scale of Javanese and Balinese gamelan music. While slendro is a pentatonic scale, pelog is commonly regarded to be a heptatonic scale. However, of the seven notes, five are considered principal notes of the scale, while two are treated as auxiliaries. At core therefore, pelog is pentatonic, the other two notes allowing for the creation of different modes of pelog. Like slendro, pelog uses a unique method of tuning. However, despite many years of research by Western ethnomusicologists, the precise method of tuning still remains something of a mystery. This sense of mystery is enhanced by the fact that every gamelan has its own particular tuning for pelog.

Selisir

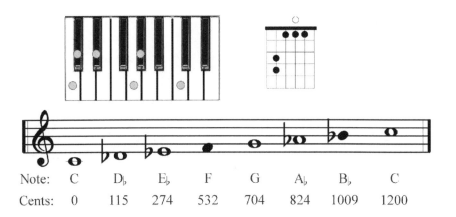

Note:	C	D♭	E♭	F	G	A♭	B♭	C
Cents:	0	115	274	532	704	824	1009	1200

Origin: Indonesia.

Scale Type: Pentatonic.

Tuning: By ear.

Styles of Music: Gamelan music.

Transposition: 1 – 2 – 4 – 1 – 4.

Features: Selisir is the main pentatonic mode of pelog, many gamelans being permanently tuned to this mode. Selisir is obtained by taking the fourth and seventh as auxiliaries. The pattern of three and two thereby produced is common to all other modes of pelog. Pentatonic modes of similar profiles are found throughout Malaysia, although not necessarily with the particularities of the Indonesian tuning.[33]

---

[33] A Burmese *Prayer Song* in a similar mode (E F G B C) is presented on p. 67 of the *New Oxford History of Music*, Vol. I.

Tembung

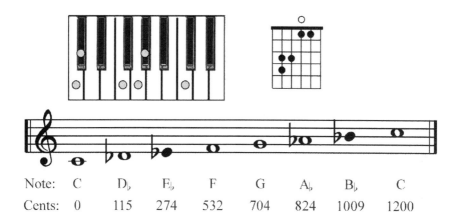

Note:	C	D♭	E♭	F	G	A♭	B♭	C
Cents:	0	115	274	532	704	824	1009	1200

Origin: Indonesia.

Scale Type: Pentatonic.

Tuning: By ear.

Styles of Music: Gamelan music.

Transposition: 1 – 4 – 2 – 1 – 4.

Features: Tembung is the second main pentatonic mode of pelog and is obtained by treating the third and seventh of pelog as auxiliaries. Tembung has a very similar profile to the Japanese kumoi joshi koto scale.

Sunaren

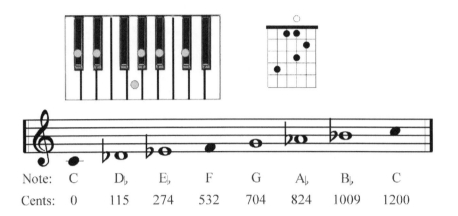

Note:	C	D♭	E♭	F	G	A♭	B♭	C
Cents:	0	115	274	532	704	824	1009	1200

Origin: Indonesia.

Scale Type: Pentatonic.

Tuning: By ear.

Styles of Music: Gamelan music.

Transposition: 2 – 4 – 1 – 2 – 3.

Features: Sunaren is the third main mode of Pelog. Sunaren can be obtained by treating the first and fourth degrees of Pelog as auxiliaries.

Slendro Gede

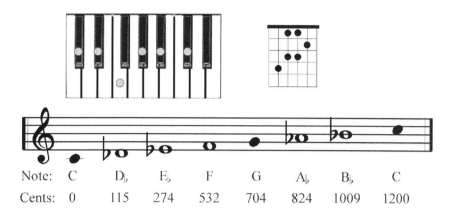

Note:	C	D♭	E♭	F	G	A♭	B♭	C
Cents:	0	115	274	532	704	824	1009	1200

Origin: Indonesia

Scale Type: Pentatonic

Tuning: By ear

Styles of Music: Gamelan music.

Transposition: 2 – 2 – 3 – 2 – 3.

Features: Since the 1980's the three main modes of pelog have been supplemented on occasion through use of other, lesser well-known modes.[34] One of these modes is slendro gede, in which the first and fifth degrees of pelog are treated as auxiliaries. Although slendro and pelog are traditionally regarded as being quite separate scale systems, slendro gede is an unusual example of a slendro mode being treated as a subset of pelog.

---

[34] See Michael Tenzer, *Gamelan Gong Kebyar: the Art of Twentieth-Century Balinese Music,* p. 29.

Baro

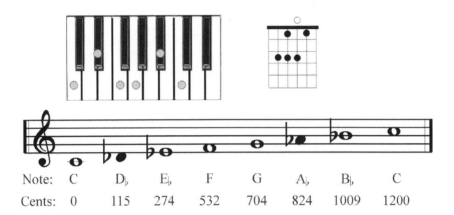

Note:	C	D♭	E♭	F	G	A♭	B♭	C
Cents:	0	115	274	532	704	824	1009	1200

Origin: Indonesia.

Scale Type: Pentatonic.

Tuning: By ear.

Styles of Music: Gamelan music.

Transposition: 3 – 2 – 2 – 3 – 2.

Features: One of the lesser well-known modes of pelog, baro treats the second and sixth degrees as auxiliaries. However, this mode is known to vary in different regions, so the scale portrayed is simply an example.[35]

---

[35] Ibid.

Pengenter

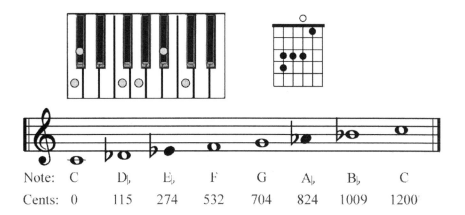

Note:	C	D♭	E♭	F	G	A♭	B♭	C
Cents:	0	115	274	532	704	824	1009	1200

Origin: Indonesia.

Scale Type: Pentatonic.

Tuning: By ear.

Styles of Music: Gamelan music.

Transposition: 1 – 4 – 2 – 3 – 2.

Features: Pengenter is also one of the lesser well-known modes of pelog[36] in which the third and sixth degrees of pelog are treated as auxiliaries.

---

[36] Ibid.

Section 10: Equatonal Scales of Thailand

As a part of mainland, Southeast Asia, Thailand shares borders with Malaysia, Cambodia, Burma and Laos. Geographically speaking, this has always put Thailand in a prime position to both receive and share musical influences with the nations that surround it. Therefore, it is not surprising perhaps, that traditional Thai music shares many traits in common with these neighboring countries. The most obvious of these is the existence of a common heritage of pentatonics, whether in hemitonic or anhemitonic forms.

Traditional Thai music tends to be ensemble oriented, three notable traditional ensembles of which are the piphat, mahori and the khruang sai. Although these ensembles differ in certain important respects, all three are united by the way in which the music is generally conceived and organized. Consisting of various horizontal layers of sound, which are combined together, we might ordinarily describe this music as being heterophonic.

However, James Morton in his very informative book on Thai traditional music takes issue with this observing that there is a great sense of multiplicity in unity within the relationship of melodies and their variants, a process which he describes as *"polyphonic stratification."*[37] Whether classified as being heterophonic or not, this technique certainly seems to suit the tuned percussion instruments – such as the gong circles and xylophones which are characteristically used in Thai ensemble music. Like much of the music of Indonesia, these metallic timbres are an important ingredient of its essential sound.

One of the most intriguing features of Thai traditional music is the musical scale that is used. This scale has seven notes that are tuned in a very particular way. The two semitones of the diatonic scale tend to be

---

[37] Ibid..

enlarged while the tones are characteristically shrunk to produce a scale whose individual steps begin to approach a uniform size. However, as with the pelog and slendro scales of Java and Bali, tuning methods are not only variable, they are also very flexible. Therefore, to expect a division of the octave into exactly seven equal parts is perhaps unreasonable.

Some of the tuned instruments are tuned using a mixture of lead and bees wax to alter their weight. The amount used is a matter of careful adjustment until the instrument 'sounds right'. Here again the sole arbiter is the ear of the musician doing the tuning. Consequently, this can never be an exact science, and while playing the instrument bits of this mixture even fall off. Suffice to say perfect equidistance is a mathematical ideal, which is not generally wanted or required in practice.

Thai Seven-toned Scale

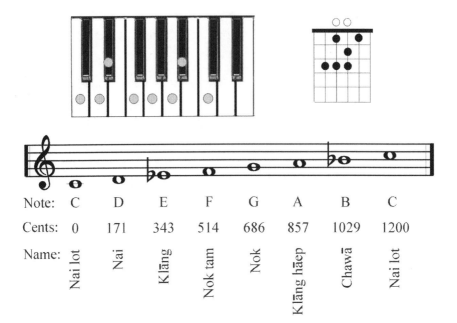

Note:	C	D	E	F	G	A	B	C
Cents:	0	171	343	514	686	857	1029	1200
Name:	Nai lot	Nai	Klāng	Nok tam	Nok	Klāng hāep	Chawā	Nai lot

Origin: Thailand.

Scale Type: Heptatonic.

Tuning: Equal seven-toned.

Styles of Music: Thai ensemble music.

Features: The Thai seven-toned scale is unique for its seeming use of an equal seven-toned division of the octave. This means that its scale steps are all more or less of uniform size, a size approximating to 171 cents – an interval which is about a third of a semitone smaller than the regular tempered whole tone of 200 cents. Shown above are the cents measurements of each of the notes of the scale, although these measurements concern an exact division of the octave into seven equal whole tones.

In practice however, do Thai musicians seek for an equal seven-toned division of the octave? Alexander Ellis helped to answer this question in his annotations to Herman Helmholtz's *On the Sensations of Tone*, where he says, "the King of Siam sent over his court band with their instruments to the London Inventions Exhibition of 1885, and the Siamese minister obligingly allowed Mr Hipkins and myself to determine the musical scale. Prince Prisdang told us that the intention was to divide the octave into seven equal intervals, each of which would then have 171.4 cents".[38]

However, Ellis's measurements of the instruments showed considerable deviations from the apparent ideal of 171 cents. Here are some of the measurements he obtained. 1) and 2) are a xylophone while 3) is a crocodile zither:

Ellis's Measurements of Thai Instruments

	1)	2)	3)
• Nai lot	0	0	0
• Nai	208	200	198
• Klāng	326	359	362
• Nok tam	537	537	528
• Nok	698	711	720
• Klāng hāep	883	883	890
• Chawā	1048	1057	1080

These show the whole tone step between degree 1 and 2 of the scale to be a fair approximation of a diatonic whole tone (204 cents). The fifths are also fair approximations of a just fifth of 702 cents. The thirds, fourth, sixths and sevenths however seem to be more or less consistently neutral. Obviously without quoting further examples of measurements of Thai instruments no strong conclusions can be drawn. All that can be observed from this is a tendency towards equidistance, which is only ever approximately realized. Naturally, this approximate realization may contribute to some of the charm and character of Thai music generally.

---

[38] Herman Helmholtz, *On the Sensations of Tone*, p. 556.

The tuning used by Thai musicians is a rather unique one, although there is evidence for shades of similar types of tuning being found on the African continent. For Ellis, grounded in the scientific acoustical theories of Helmholtz, Thai tuning appeared to be unnatural in terms of the way in which it appeared to flout acoustic norms.[39] Yet those norms generally derive from instruments built from tubes, pipes and strings which tend to vibrate harmonically. Instruments of fixed tuning in Thai ensembles such as xylophones and kettle gongs do not vibrate in the same way, there being plenty of inharmonic partials in the mix. This in itself obviates any necessity for tuning instruments with respect to strictly harmonic principles.

A further feature is the style of polyphonic *stratification*, which Morton refers to in his characterization of Thai traditional music. The impulse behind this style is essentially horizontal rather than vertical. There is consequently no need to regulate the tuning of the notes of the scale in such a way as to produce consonant harmonies. The precedents for this style undoubtedly have their origins in nature and processes of natural observation. If we listen to the birds of the forest singing, the result will be a similar polyphonic stratification – many different layers of sound being combined together simultaneously. No expectancy is present for the birds to sing in harmony. There is no sense of harmony, except for the sheer sensual beauty of all of the individual lines and layers of bird song, every one being different, yet somehow blending.

With this essentially horizontal mode of perception of sound, tonal colour plays a more important part than a sense of harmony. Each birdsong or call has its own particular tonal colour within the overall mix of colours. Moreover, it is particularly absorbing to pick out one such thread of colour – the song of a particular bird. Thai music is very similar. It is equally absorbing to pick out one layer of the music and to focus upon that. In doing so, the other layers tend to recede into the background, forming as it were a pleasant commentary upon the layer that is being focused upon.

---

[39] David Morton, *The Traditional Music of Thailand*, p. 27.

Thai Mode I

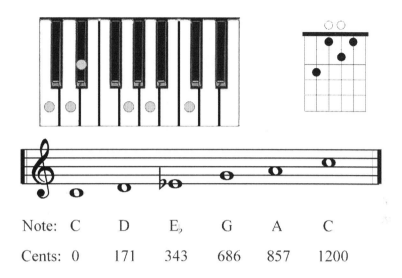

Note:	C	D	E♭	G	A	C
Cents:	0	171	343	686	857	1200

Origin: Thailand.

Scale Type: Pentatonic.

Tuning: Equal seven-toned.

Styles of Music: Thai ensemble music.

Transposition: 2 – 1 – 4 – 2 – 3.

Features: Although Thai musician use a seven-toned scale, not all seven of the notes are used within a given composition. Mostly five are used, or on occasion six. Moreover, where more than five are used, the extra one or two notes are often used simply as occasional decorations. In this respect, the Thai seven-toned scale is very similar to the Indonesian *pelog*. In effect, this means that the same argument could perhaps be applied to the Thai scale – it is not really a seven-toned scale, but a five-toned scale with two extra-notes provided in order to facilitate processes of modal selection and *metabole* (change of mode).

The relationship between the five tones of a mode and the seven notes of the foundation scale is a familiar one to be found throughout East Asia. The notes of the pentatonic mode form a three and two pattern. Between the group of three and two lies a 'gap' within which lies the two thirds of the pentatonic scale. In Thai music there are four such pentatonic modes typically used. In the first mode, the fourth and seventh steps of the seven-toned scale are treated as auxiliaries. This means that they are either not referred to in the music, touched upon only briefly, or else used for the specific purposes of modulation (metabole):

Thai Mode 2

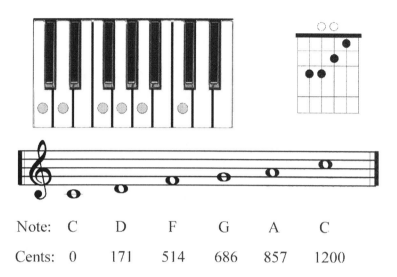

Note:	C	D	F	G	A	C
Cents:	0	171	514	686	857	1200

Origin: Thailand.

Scale Type: Pentatonic.

Tuning: Equal seven-toned.

Styles of Music: Thai ensemble music.

Transposition: 2 – 3 – 2 – 2 – 3.

Features: Of the seven original notes of the Thai seven-toned scale, five are chosen to be the principal notes, while two are treated as auxiliaries. In the second pentatonic mode, the third and seventh are treated as auxiliaries.

Thai Mode 3

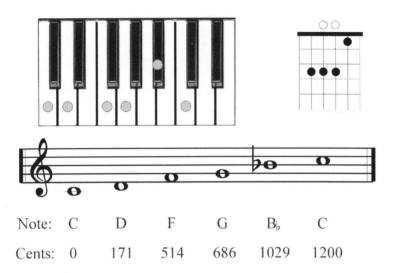

Note:	C	D	F	G	B♭	C
Cents:	0	171	514	686	1029	1200

Origin: Thailand.

Scale Type: Pentatonic.

Tuning: Equal seven-toned.

Styles of Music: Thai ensemble music.

Transposition: 2 – 3 – 2 – 3 – 2.

Features: Of the seven original notes of the Thai seven-toned scale, five are chosen to be the principal notes, while two are treated as auxiliaries. In this third pentatonic mode, the third and sixth are treated as auxiliaries.

Thai Mode 4

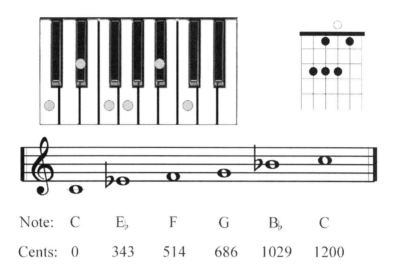

Note:	C	E♭	F	G	B♭	C
Cents:	0	343	514	686	1029	1200

Origin: Thailand.

Scale Type: Pentatonic.

Tuning: Equal seven-toned.

Styles of Music: Thai ensemble music.

Transposition: 3 – 2 – 2 – 3 – 2.

Features: Of the seven original notes of the Thai seven-toned scale, five are chosen to be the principal notes, while two are treated as auxiliaries. In this fourth pentatonic mode, the second and sixth are treated as auxiliaries.

Section 11: Kora Scales of Western Africa

The kora is a type of bridge harp with 21 strings arranged in two side rows. The instrument is built around a gourd resonating chamber with a long upright hardwood neck that stands vertically. The kora produces a beautiful ethereal sound which is somewhere between a harp and a classical guitar. It is a relatively recent instrument dating back only a couple of hundred years.

Played in Gambia, Mali, Guinea, the Ivory Coast and Senegal, the kora developed as an important instrument of the jalis, hereditary musicians attached to the royal courts. Probably due to its beautiful euphonious sound, the kora has now become an extremely popular instrument, frequently heard in popular music contexts, both at home and abroad.

The kora is ordinarily heard accompanying a singer, although it is also popular as a solo instrument. It is played using a combination of two basic techniques, kumbengo, which involves the playing of ostinato riffs heard as an accompaniment to the voice, and birimintingo, flamboyant and often brilliant improvised flourishes of melody.

The kora has a range of just over three octaves of a heptatonic scale. Today it is becoming increasingly common to tune the kora using Western tempered methods of tuning. This enables the kora to play along with Western instruments, although traditionally, a variety of fascinating tunings are used, which actually vary between the different regions in which the kora is played. These individual tunings help to give the kora music of those regions its own unique sense of individuality and identity.

Silaba

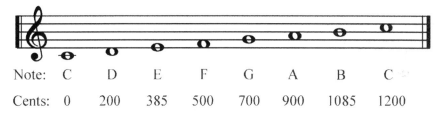

Note:	C	D	E	F	G	A	B	C
Cents:	0	200	385	500	700	900	1085	1200

Origin: West Africa.

Scale Type: Heptatonic.

Tuning: Just[40].

Styles of Music: Kora harp.

Transposition: 2 – 2 – 1 – 2 – 2 – 2 – 1.

Features: As played by musicians of Gambia, Mali, Senegal and the Ivory Coast, the kora is now attaining a popularity that belies its origins as a local West African instrument. Silaba is the standard tuning for the kora, a scale that appears to be a simple major scale. We can however note a significant difference. The major third and seventh are tuned about 15 cents lower than their equal tempered counterparts. This brings them into the range of the pure intervals of the major third (5/4) - 386 cents - and the major seventh (15/8) - 1088 cents. This use of just intervals in this way helps to explain the beautiful mellow quality of Silaba.

Tomora Mesengo

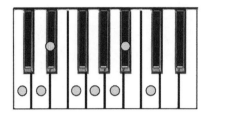

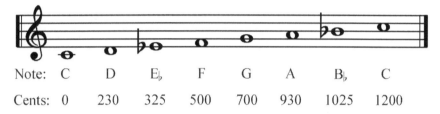

Note:	C	D	E♭	F	G	A	B♭	C
Cents:	0	230	325	500	700	930	1025	1200

Origin: West Africa.

Scale Type: Heptatonic.

Tuning: Just.

Styles of Music: Kora harp.

Transposition: 2 – 1 – 2 – 2 – 2 – 1 – 2.

Features: Tomara Mesengo is a kora tuning popular in East Gambia. Distinctive are the large whole tone of 230 cents and the minor third of 325 cents. The nearest historical tuning to this is the soft diatonic genera recommended by Ptolemy for the tuning of the ancient Greek lyre.

---

[40] The tunings for the kora scales given in this section are recommended in Anthony King's informative study of the construction of the kora and its tuning (1972). For more information on this see the section Recommended Reading.

Sauta

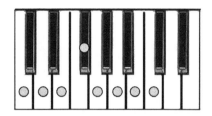

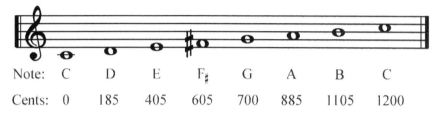

Note:	C	D	E	F♯	G	A	B	C
Cents:	0	185	405	605	700	885	1105	1200

Origin: West Africa.

Scale Type: Heptatonic.

Tuning: Just.

Styles of Music: Kora harp.

Transposition: 2 – 2 – 2 – 1 – 2 – 2 – 1.

Features: Sauta resembles the modern Lydian mode, bar for a few significant differences. The semitone is smaller (95 cents) while the tones are of two sizes – the minor tone of 185 cents and large whole tone of 220 cents. As a type of diatonic tuning, the nearest equivalent is an ancient Greek lyre tuning: Aristoxenus' diatonic with hemiolic chromatic diesis.

Hardino

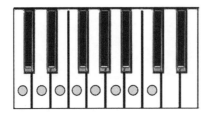

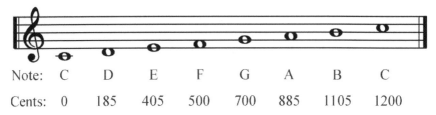

Note:	C	D	E	F	G	A	B	C
Cents:	0	185	405	500	700	885	1105	1200

Origin:　　　　West Africa.

Scale Type:　　Heptatonic.

Tuning:　　　　Just.

Styles of Music:　Kora harp.

Transposition:　2 – 2 – 1 – 2 – 2 – 2 – 1.

Features: Hardino is one of the favored tunings used by the kora players of Mali. Although appearing to be a different tuning, it is simply another modal position of Tomara Mesengo. When the third degree of Tomara Mesengo is taken to be the tonic Hardino results.

Section 12: Scales of Northern India

The musical scales of Indian classical music, long ago reached a stage of sophistication and perfection that makes the scales used in the West look crude by comparison. Because of this, it is not even possible for a Western musician to make authentic use of these scales without special training. Connected with this is the idea of the rāg, a framework for melodic improvisation used by Indian classical musicians. To make effective use of such frameworks entails a long period of study, learning and contemplation in order to master the particular characteristics of rāg. Once mastered, a judgment of the musician's realization of a given rag will then be made by an educated audience well versed in the language of rāg themselves.

Suffice to say, it is not really possible for a Western musician to pick this up in a short period of time. That said, in the West there is a significant interest in the scales used in Indian classical music. This interest often stems from a desire to experiment with such scales in order to produce a particular feeling, atmosphere or mood – an art in which Indian classical musicians are absolute experts.

The scales that Western musicians have used in this respect fall into two main categories; there are the scales of Northern Indian classical music and the scales of Southern Indian or Carnatic music. In this section, we will consider the scales of Northern Indian classical music which are called that. However, we need to bear in mind that Indian classical musicians do not use thāt as musical scales for composition, but rather as a convenient way of grouping and categorizing rāg s according to their scalar material. There are such ten such thāt which were originally formulated by the Indian theorist Vishnu Narayan Bhatkhande (1860 – 1936). This next section will cover these ten scales, together with their properties and characteristics.

Bilawal Thāt

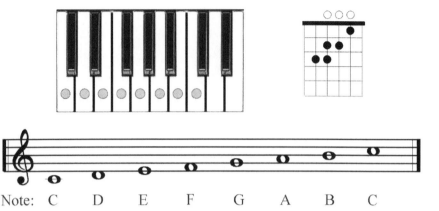

Note: C   D   E   F   G   A   B   C

Origin: India

Scale Type: Heptatonic

Tuning: Just intonation

Styles of Music: Northern Hindustani classical music.

Transposition: 2 – 2 – 1 – 2 – 2 – 2 – 1.

Features: The thāt system was devised by the Hindu theorist Vishnu Bhatkande (1860 – 1936) as a way of organizing rāgs into related groups. Thāts in this sense are parent scales under whose umbrella a wide range of different rāgs can be embraced. In terms of Bilawal Thāt, this includes important rāgs such as Bilawal, Lachasak, Durga, Pahari and Sankhara.

Bilawal thāt is a species of diatonic mode that has a similar profile to the Western major scale or, the modern Ionian mode.

Kalyan Thãt

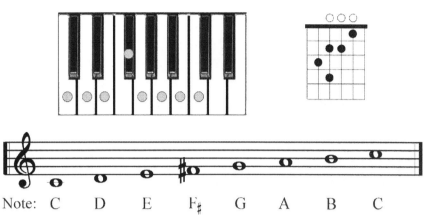

Note: C   D   E   F♯   G   A   B   C

Origin: India

Scale Type: Heptatonic

Tuning: Just intonation

Styles of Music: Northern Hindustani classical music.

Transposition: 2 – 2 – 2 – 1 – 2 – 2 – 1.

Features: Like Bilawal Thãt, Kalyan is a type of diatonic mode. The difference lies in Kalyan's sharp fourth, which gives it a similar profile to the modern Western Lydian mode. Some of the famous rãgs that belong to this group are Kalyan, Gaura Saranga, Suddha Saranga, Hemanta and Hindol.

Khamaj Thãt

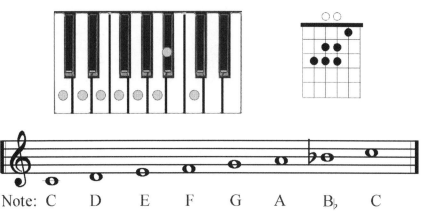

Note: C   D   E   F   G   A   B♭   C

Origin: India

Scale Type: Heptatonic

Tuning: Just intonation

Styles of Music: Northern Hindustani classical music.

Transposition: 2 – 2 – 1 – 2 – 2 – 1 – 2.

Features: Khamaj thãt is another type of diatonic mode. The flat seventh reveals it to be very similar to the Western Mixolydian mode. Some of the famous rãgs that belong to this thãt are Khamaj, Tilanga, Jhinjhoti, Bangala and Madhyamad Saranga

Khafi Thãt

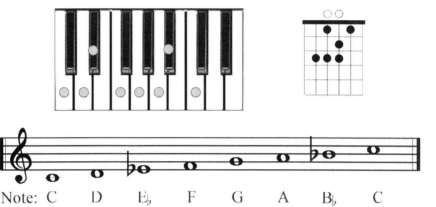

Note: C   D   E♭   F   G   A   B♭   C

Origin: India

Scale Type: Heptatonic

Tuning: Just intonation

Styles of Music: Northern Hindustani classical music.

Transposition: 2 – 1 – 2 – 2 – 2 – 1 – 2.

Features: In Khafi thãt the third and seventh appear in flat or komal position. This produces another species of diatonic mode corresponding to the Western Dorian mode. In former times, musicians considered Khafi to be the basic scale rather than Bilawal as they do today. Some of the well-known rãgs that belong to this thãt are Khafi, Desi, Bhimpalasi, Megha and Abhogi.

Asavari Thāt

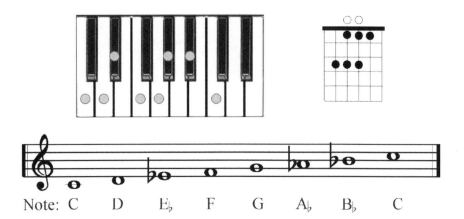

Note: C D E♭ F G A♭ B♭ C

Origin: India

Scale Type: Heptatonic

Tuning: Just intonation

Styles of Music: Northern Hindustani classical music.

Transposition: 2 – 1 – 2 – 2 – 1 – 2 – 2.

Features: In Asavari thāt, the third, sixth and seventh appear in their flat or komal position. This produces a diatonic modal scale that is similar to the Western natural minor mode or modern Aeolian mode. Some of the rāgs that belong to this thāt are Asavari, Katyayani, Ghandari, Jaunpuri and Sarang Asavari.

Bhairavi Thāt

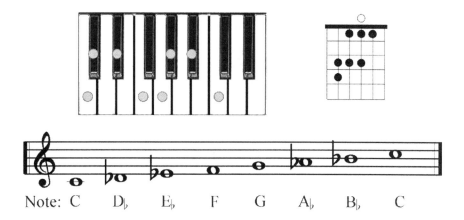

Note: C   D♭   E♭   F   G   A♭   B♭   C

Origin: India

Scale Type: Heptatonic

Tuning: Just intonation

Styles of Music: Northern Hindustani classical music.

Transposition: 1 – 2 – 2 – 2 – 1 – 2 – 2.

Features: In Bhairavi thāt the second, third, sixth and seventh degrees all appear in their flat or komal position. This produces another species of diatonic mode that would be identified in the west as the Phrygian mode. Some of the rāgs that belong to this thāt are Bhairavi, Malkauns, Dhanssree, Nandkaus and Rāgamanjari

Purvi Thãt

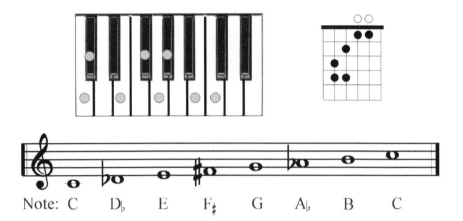

Note: C   D♭   E   F♯   G   A♭   B   C

Origin: India

Scale Type: Heptatonic

Tuning: Just intonation

Styles of Music: Northern Hindustani classical music.

Transposition: 1 – 3 – 2 – 1 – 1 – 3 – 1.

Features: Purvi thãt uses a sharp fourth that alters the profile of the lower tetrachord. Instead of spanning a perfect fourth, it now spans an augmented fourth. Using as they do the intervals of a semitone and augmented tone, the lower and upper tetrachords are both chromatic. This produces a very distinctive modal scale that is not generally recognized in Western music. Some of the rãgs that belong to this thãt are Purvi, Ahir Lalita, Kumari, Basanta and Paraj.

Todi Thãt

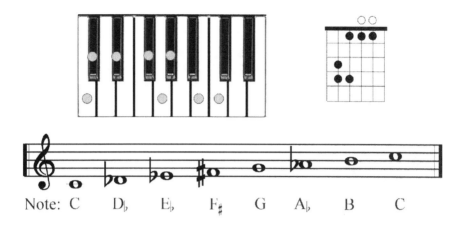

Note: C D♭ E♭ F♯ G A♭ B C

Origin: India

Scale Type: Heptatonic

Tuning: Just intonation

Styles of Music: Northern Hindustani classical music.

Transposition: 1 – 2 – 3 – 1 – 1 – 3 – 1.

Features: Todi thãt has a very strong and recognizable profile due to the use of a sharp fourth, the augmented second between the third and the fourth, and the chromatic upper tetrachord. This produces a scale that is unique to Indian music. Some of the rãgs that belong to this thãt are Todi, Multani, Lilavati, Bhupala Todi and Shivraj.

Bhairav Thãt

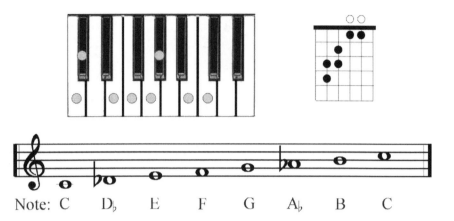

Note: C   D♭   E   F   G   A♭   B   C

Origin: India

Scale Type: Heptatonic

Tuning: Just intonation

Styles of Music: Northern Hindustani classical music.

Transposition: 1 – 3 – 1 – 2 – 1 – 3 – 1.

Features: Bhairav thãt uses both an upper and a lower chromatic tetrachord. As such, it has a very similar profile to the Western double harmonic scale. Some of the rãgs that belong to this thãt are Bhairav, Jangala, Araj, Bhankara and Saveri.

Marwa Thãt

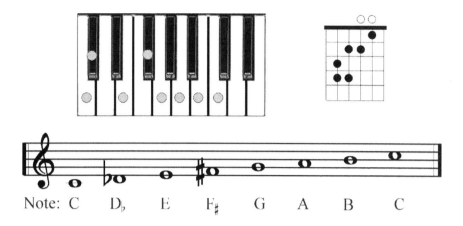

Note: C D♭ E F♯ G A B C

Origin: India

Scale Type: Heptatonic

Tuning: Just intonation

Styles of Music: Northern Hindustani classical music.

Transposition: 1 – 3 – 2 – 1 – 2 – 2 – 1.

Features: Marwa thãt offers a very distinctive mix of modal influences. The fourth is sharp, the lower tetrachord is chromatic and the upper tetrachord is diatonic. This gives Marwa a very distinctive modal profile that is again, unique to Indian music. Some of the rãgs that belong to this thãt are Marwa, Bhankar, Puriya, Pancham and Bhatiyara

Section 13: Scales of Carnatic Music

The ten thãt of Northern Indian classical music are one group of scales associated with Indian classical music in general. Another important group of scales is those used in Southern Indian or Carnatic music, called mela. There are seventy-two of these, within whose range we find not only versions of most of the scales that have been used in Western music, but many more besides, scales which are probably unique to the history of world music.

Western musicians who come across this modal system are often surprised to find in this group of scales a wealth of scalar material literally undreamed of in the West. In this section, we will consider each of the seventy-two mela, together with their properties, characteristics and any resemblances to other scales generally. Presenting these within a Western format makes it easier for a Western musician to quickly grasp and play such scales should they wish to. Naturally, should a musician want to explore these scales at a deeper level, they will then need to find a genuine teacher of Carnatic music.

Before introducing these scales individually there are a number of concepts that help us to appreciate how the seventy-two mela are organized and arranged. The main concept involved is the tetrachord. Rather than viewing a scale as a ladder of seven notes stretched between the extremes of an octave, Carnatic music approaches scales after the ancient Greek fashion, which is as a sum of two tetrachords, one lower and one upper, each tetrachord spanning a fourth. For illustration purposes, the Western major scale viewed in this way would appear as in the following illustration:

Western Major Scale as Sum of Two Tetrachords

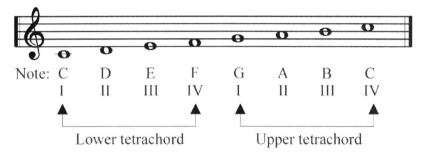

Carnatic music recognizes two main types of tetrachord, diatonic and chromatic. Diatonic tetrachords are composed of two tones and a semitone, which can be arranged in three ways:

I: Tone, tone, semitone.

II: Tone, semitone, tone.

III: Semitone, tone, tone.

Chromatic tetrachords are composed of two semitones and an augmented tone. These can also be arranged in three ways:

I: Semitone, semitone, augmented tone.

II: Semitone, augmented tone, semitone.

III: Augmented tone, semitone, semitone.

Consequently, six types of tetrachord are recognized, three diatonic and three chromatic.

As a scale of seven notes is composed of two tetrachords means that there are thus six times six or thirty-six basic seven note scales. These thirty-six scales are then supplemented by another group of thirty-six scales in which the fourth of the lower tetrachord is sharp. An example of a scale from the West that uses a sharp fourth in this way is the Lydian mode, while another is the Hungarian minor mode. These two examples are perhaps enough to show the felt necessity amongst musicians from any part of the world for including a group of scales that use a sharp fourth. The total number of scales belonging to the mela system is therefore twice thirty-six or seventy-two.

For convenience, these seventy-two scales are arranged into twelve groups or chakras of six scales each. The chakras themselves are names applied to mela that all share the same type of lower tetrachord. As there are six types of upper tetrachord, means that there are therefore six mela in each chakra.

We will now consider the seventy-two mela individually, beginning with the first chakra called Indu.

Mela Kanakangi

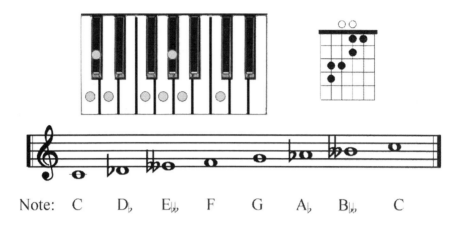

Note: C   D♭   E♭♭   F   G   A♭   B♭♭   C

Origin: Carnatic.

Scale Type: Heptatonic.

Tuning: Just.

Chakra: Indu.

Number: 1/72.

Transposition: 1 – 1 – 3 – 2 – 1 – 1 – 3.

Features: Kanakangi uses both chromatic lower and upper tetrachords. The nearest equivalent to this mode that we know of is the ancient Greek chromatic genus, mela Kanakangi corresponding with the ancient Greek chromatic Dorian mode. In more specifically modern terms, Kanakangi resembles a Phrygian mode the third and seventh of which have been flattened.

Mela Ratnangi

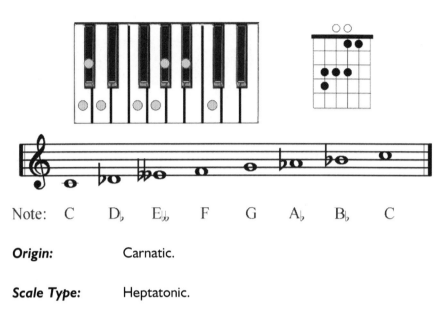

Note: C   D♭   E♭♭   F   G   A♭   B♭   C

Origin: Carnatic.

Scale Type: Heptatonic.

Tuning: Just.

Chakra: Indu.

Number: 2/72.

Transposition: 1 – 1 – 3 – 2 – 1 – 2 – 2.

Features: Ratnangi has a chromatic lower tetrachord and a diatonic upper tetrachord. Ratnangi is one of the modes that is unique to the mela system. A Western musician might think of this mode as a Phrygian mode, the third of which has been flattened.

Mela Ganamurti

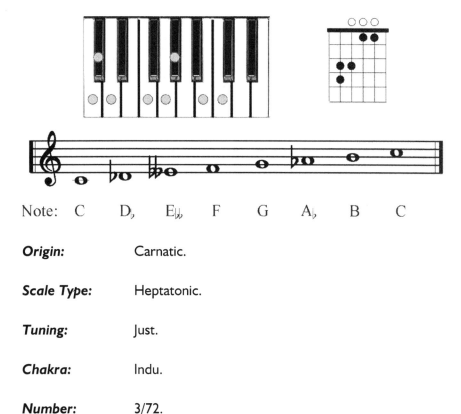

Note: C   D♭   E♭♭   F   G   A♭   B   C

Origin: Carnatic.

Scale Type: Heptatonic.

Tuning: Just.

Chakra: Indu.

Number: 3/72.

Transposition: 1 – 1 – 3 – 2 – 1 – 3 – 1.

Features: Ganamurti uses a chromatic lower and upper tetrachord. As such, Ganamurti is a type of chromatic mode. Ganamurti is also one of the modes unique to the mela system.

Mela Vanaspati

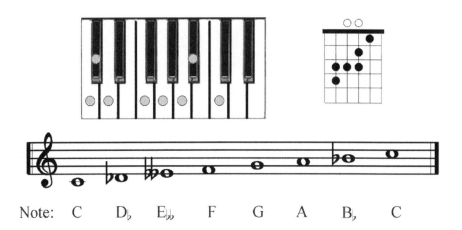

Note: C   D♭   E♭♭   F   G   A   B♭   C

Origin: Carnatic.

Scale Type: Heptatonic.

Tuning: Just.

Chakra: Indu.

Number: 4/72.

Transposition: 1 – 1 – 3 – 2 – 2 – 1 – 2.

Features: Vanaspati uses a chromatic lower tetrachord and a diatonic upper tetrachord. Vanaspati is one of the modes unique to the mela system.

Mela Manavati

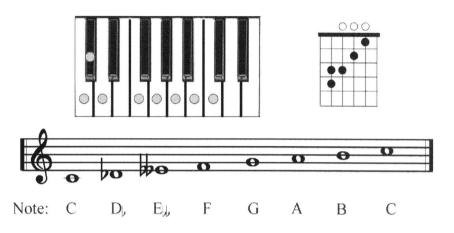

Note: C   D♭   E♭♭   F   G   A   B   C

Origin: Carnatic.

Scale Type: Heptatonic.

Tuning: Just.

Chakra: Indu.

Number: 5/72.

Transposition: 1 – 1 – 3 – 2 – 2 – 2 – 1.

Features: Manavati is a mixed chromatic and diatonic mode, using a chromatic lower tetrachord and a diatonic upper tetrachord. Manavati is one of the modes unique to the mela system.

Mela Tanarupi

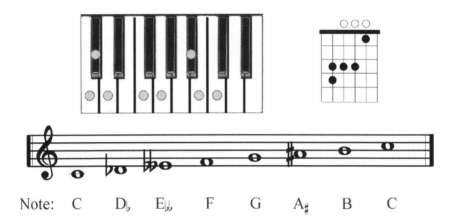

Note: C   D♭   E♭♭   F   G   A♯   B   C

Origin: Carnatic.

Scale Type: Heptatonic.

Tuning: Just.

Chakra: Indu.

Number: 6/72.

Transposition: 1 – 1 – 3 – 2 – 3 – 1 – 1.

Features: Tanarupi uses both a lower and an upper chromatic tetrachord. As such, Tanarupi is a type of chromatic mode. Observe that it is non-invertible, the transposition figures (1 – 1 – 3 – 2 – 3 – 1 – 1) reading the same forward as backward. Tanarupi is one of the modes unique to the mela system.

Mela Senavati

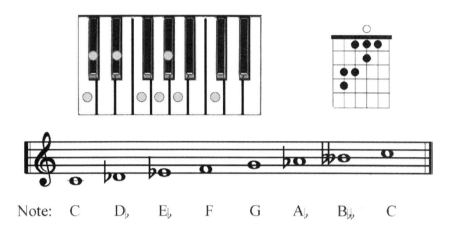

Note: C   D♭   E♭   F   G   A♭   B♭♭   C

Origin: Carnatic

Scale Type: Heptatonic.

Tuning: Just.

Chakra: Netra.

Number: 7/72.

Transposition: 1 – 2 – 2 – 2 – 1 – 1 – 3.

Features: Mela belonging to the Netra chakra all have a Phrygian lower tetrachord – semitone, tone and tone. The main feature of Senavati is the chromatic upper tetrachord. Senavati is one of the modes unique to the mela system. A Western musician might think of this mode as a Phrygian mode with flattened seventh.

Mela Hanumatodi

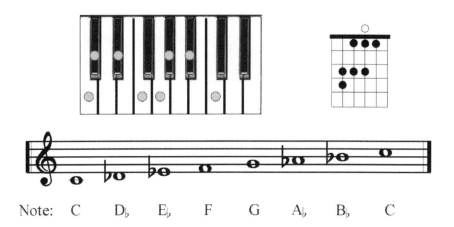

Note: C   D♭   E♭   F   G   A♭   B♭   C

Origin: Carnatic

Scale Type: Heptatonic.

Tuning: Just.

Chakra: Netra.

Number: 8/72.

Transposition: 1 – 2 – 2 – 2 – 1 – 2 – 2.

Features: Hanumatodi uses both upper and lower diatonic tetrachords. It is a species of diatonic mode, equivalents of which can be found in the ancient Greek Dorian mode, also known as the modern Western Phrygian mode, the Japanese In scale, Maqam Kurd, Bhairavi thāt of Northern Hindustani music and among Jewish prayer modes, Yishtabach.

Mela Dhenuka

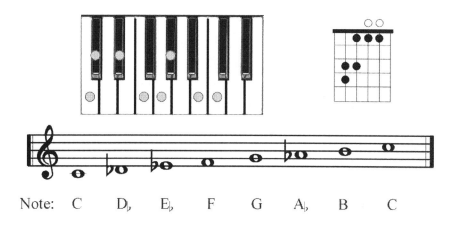

Note: C   D♭   E♭   F   G   A♭   B   C

Origin: Carnatic

Scale Type: Heptatonic.

Tuning: Just.

Chakra: Netra.

Number: 9/72.

Transposition: 1 – 2 – 2 – 2 – 1 – 3 – 1.

Features: Dennuka uses a diatonic lower and a chromatic upper tetrachord. It is very similar to the harmonic Phrygian mode of modern Western classical music, or maqam Shahnaz Kurdi of Arabic modal music.

Mela Natakapriya

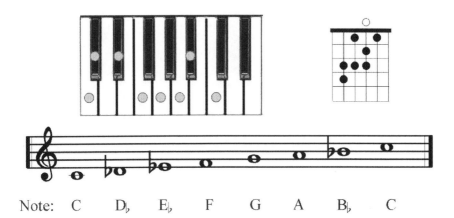

Note: C   D♭   E♭   F   G   A   B♭   C

Origin: Carnatic

Scale Type: Heptatonic.

Tuning: Just.

Chakra: Netra.

Number: 10/72.

Transposition: 1 – 2 – 2 – 2 – 2 – 1 – 2.

Features: Natakapriya uses both diatonic lower and upper tetrachords. The nearest equivalent in Western music is the Neapolitan Dorian mode, that is a Dorian mode the second of which has been flattened.

Mela Kokilapriya

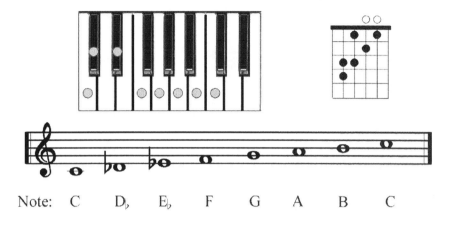

Note: C   D♭   E♭   F   G   A   B   C

Origin: Carnatic

Scale Type: Heptatonic.

Tuning: Just.

Chakra: Netra.

Number: 11/72.

Transposition: 1 − 2 − 2 − 2 − 2 − 2 − 1.

Features: Kokilapriya uses diatonic lower and upper tetrachords. It closely resembles the non-invertible Phrygian major mode of modern Western classical music and jazz.

Mela Rupavati

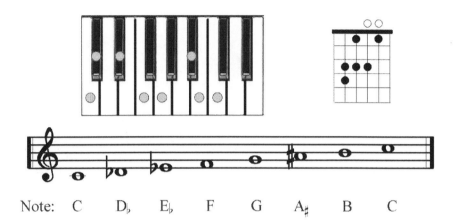

Note: C   D♭   E♭   F   G   A♯   B   C

Origin: Carnatic

Scale Type: Heptatonic.

Tuning: Just.

Chakra: Netra.

Number: 12/72.

Transposition: 1 – 2 – 2 – 2 – 1 – 3 – 1.

Features: Rupavati uses a diatonic lower and chromatic upper tetrachord. This makes it a mixed mode that resembles a harmonic Phrygian mode with raised sixth. Rupavati is one of the modes that is unique to the mela system.

Mela Gayakapriya

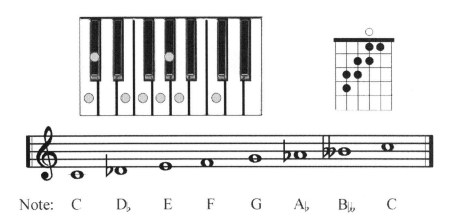

Note: C   D♭   E   F   G   A♭   B♭♭   C

Origin: Carnatic

Scale Type: Heptatonic.

Tuning: Just.

Chakra: Agni.

Number: 13/72.

Transposition: 1 – 3 – 1 – 2 – 1 – 1 – 3.

Features: The six Mela belonging to the Agni chakra all have a chromatic lower tetrachord of the type semitone, augmented tone, and semitone. Gayakapriya uses both lower and upper chromatic tetrachords. Gayakapriya is one of the modes unique to the mela system.

Mela Vakulabharanam

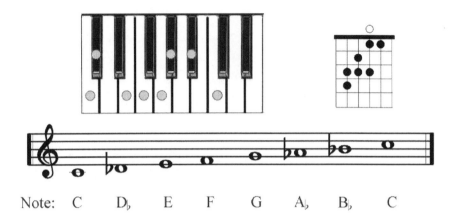

Note: C   D♭   E   F   G   A♭   B♭   C

Origin: Carnatic

Scale Type: Heptatonic.

Tuning: Just.

Chakra: Agni.

Number: 14/72.

Transposition: 1 – 3 – 1 – 2 – 1 – 2 – 2.

Features: Vakulabharanam uses a chromatic lower and a diatonic upper tetrachord. The nearest Western equivalents are the Spanish Phrygian mode of Western music, Ahavah Rabbah of Klezmer (the *Havah Nagila* mode) and Maqam Hijaz (descending form) of Arabic modal music.

Mela Mayamalavagowla

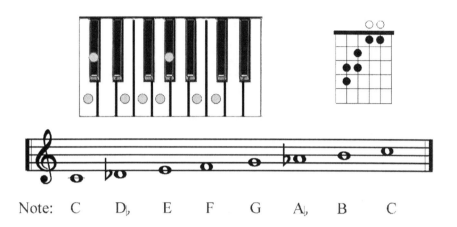

Note: C   D♭   E   F   G   A♭   B   C

Origin: Carnatic

Scale Type: Heptatonic.

Tuning: Just.

Chakra: Agni.

Number: 15/72.

Transposition: 1 – 3 – 1 – 2 – 1 – 3 – 1.

Features: Mayamalavagowla is a form of chromatic mode, using both lower and upper chromatic tetrachords. It is similar to the double harmonic scale of modern Western music, Maqam Shahnaz of Arabic modal music and Bhairav thāt of Northern Hindustani music.

Mela Chakravakam

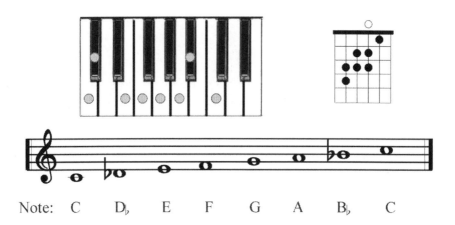

Note: C   D♭   E   F   G   A   B♭   C

Origin: Carnatic.

Scale Type: Heptatonic.

Tuning: Just.

Chakra: Agni.

Number: 16/72.

Transposition: 1 – 3 – 1 – 2 – 2 – 1 – 2.

Features: Chakravakham uses a chromatic lower and diatonic upper tetrachord. The nearest equivalents are the Neapolitan Mixolydian mode of modern Western music or Maqam Zankulah of Arabic modal music.

Mela Suryakantam

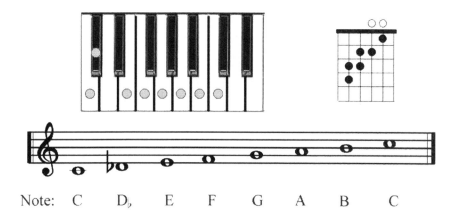

Note: C   D♭   E   F   G   A   B   C

Origin: Carnatic

Scale Type: Heptatonic.

Tuning: Just.

Chakra: Agni.

Number: 17/72.

Transposition: 1 – 3 – 1 – 2 – 2 – 2 – 1.

Features: Suryakantam uses a lower chromatic and diatonic upper tetrachord. The nearest equivalent in Western music is the Neapolitan major mode.

Mela Hatakambari

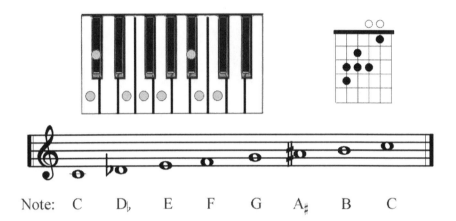

Note: C   D♭   E   F   G   A♯   B   C

Origin: Carnatic

Scale Type: Heptatonic.

Tuning: Just.

Chakra: Agni.

Number: 18/72.

Transposition: 1 – 3 – 1 – 2 – 3 – 1 – 1.

Features: Hatakambari uses both lower and upper chromatic tetrachords. Hatakambari is one of the modes unique to the mela system.

Mela Jhankaradhwani

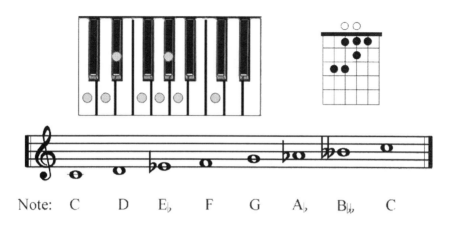

Note:	C	D	E♭	F	G	A♭	B♭♭	C

Origin: Carnatic.

Scale Type: Heptatonic.

Tuning: Just.

Chakra: Veda.

Number: 19/72.

Transposition: 2 – 1 – 2 – 2 – 1 – 1 – 3.

Features: Jhankaradhwani is the first of the six mela belonging to the Veda chakra. Mela belonging to the Veda chakra all use a minor diatonic lower tetrachord. In the case of Jhankaradhwani, the mode is completed through the addition of a chromatic tetrachord. Jhankaradhwani is one of the unique modes belonging to the mela system

Mela Natabhairavi

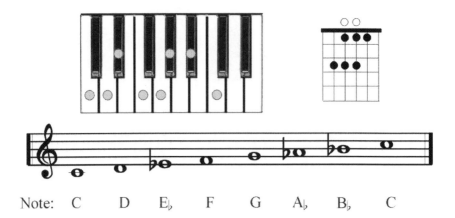

Note: C   D   E♭   F   G   A♭   B♭   C

Origin: Carnatic.

Scale Type: Heptatonic.

Tuning: Just.

Chakra: Veda.

Number: 20/72.

Transposition: 2 – 1 – 2 – 2 – 1 – 2 – 2.

Features: Natabhairavi is a type of diatonic mode the nearest equivalents to which are the Ancient Greek Hypodorian Mode, the modern Western Aeolian or natural minor mode, Asavari thāt of Northern Hindustani music and Maqam Nahawand Kurd of Arabic modal music..

Mela Keeravani

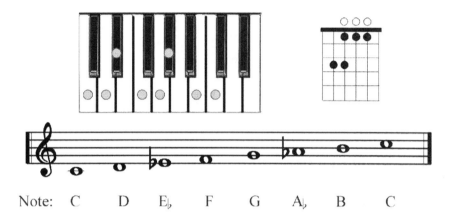

Note: C   D   E♭   F   G   A♭   B   C

Origin: Carnatic.

Scale Type: Heptatonic.

Tuning: Just.

Chakra: Veda.

Number: 21/72.

Transposition: 2 – 1 – 2 – 2 – 1 – 3 – 1.

Features: Keeravani uses a diatonic lower and chromatic upper tetrachord. The nearest equivalent in the West is the harmonic minor scale.

Mela Kharaharapriya

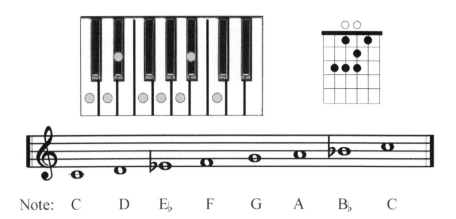

Note: C   D   E♭   F   G   A   B♭   C

Origin: Carnatic.

Scale Type: Heptatonic.

Tuning: Just.

Chakra: Veda.

Number: 22/72.

Transposition: 2 – 1 – 2 – 2 – 2 – 1 – 2.

Features: Kharaharapriya is a type of diatonic mode the nearest equivalents to which are the ancient Greek Phrygian mode, the modern Western Dorian mode, maqam Nahawand Kabir of Arabic modal music, and Khafi Thāt of Northern Hindustani music.

Mela Gourimanohari

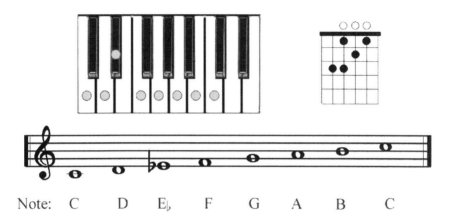

Note: C   D   E♭   F   G   A   B   C

Origin: Carnatic.

Scale Type: Heptatonic.

Tuning: Just.

Chakra: Veda.

Number: 23/72.

Transposition: 2 – 1 – 2 – 2 – 2 – 2 – 1.

Features: Gourimanohari is similar to the melodic minor scale in its ascending form, otherwise known as the jazz minor scale. It also resembles maqam Tarz Jadid of Arabic modal music.

Mela Varunapriya

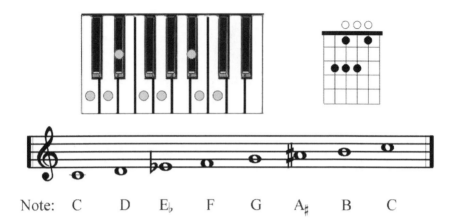

Note: C   D   E♭   F   G   A♯   B   C

Origin: Carnatic.

Scale Type: Heptatonic.

Tuning: Just.

Chakra: Veda.

Number: 24/72.

Transposition: 2 – 1 – 2 – 2 – 3 – 1 – 1.

Features: Varunapriya uses a diatonic lower and chromatic upper tetrachord. Varunapriya is one of the modes unique to the mela system.

Mela Mararanjani

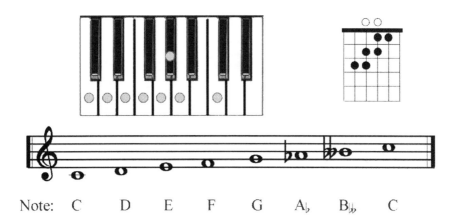

Note: C   D   E   F   G   A♭   B♭♭   C

Origin: Carnatic.

Scale Type: Heptatonic.

Tuning: Just.

Chakra: Bana.

Number: 25/72.

Transposition: 2 – 2 – 1 – 2 – 1 – 1 – 3.

Features: Mararanjani is the first mela of the Bana chakra. All six mela belonging to the Bana chakra uses a major diatonic lower tetrachord. Mararanjani completes the mode by adding a chromatic upper tetrachord. Mararanjani is one of the modes unique to the mela system.

Mela Charukesi

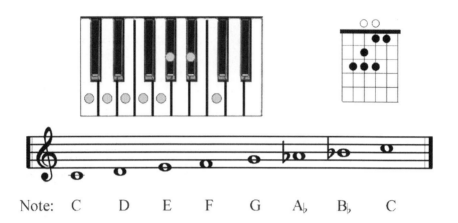

Note: C   D   E   F   G   A♭   B♭   C

Origin: Carnatic.

Scale Type: Heptatonic.

Tuning: Just.

Chakra: Bana.

Number: 26/72.

Transposition: 2 – 2 – 1 – 2 – 1 – 2 – 2.

Features: Charukesi uses both lower and upper diatonic tetrachords. It resembles the major-minor mode or alternatively the Mixolydian mode with flat sixth, of modern Western music.

Mela Sarasangi

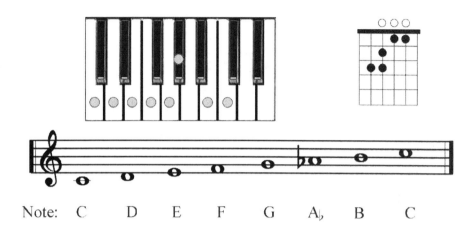

Note: C   D   E   F   G   A♭   B   C

Origin: Carnatic.

Scale Type: Heptatonic.

Tuning: Just.

Chakra: Bana.

Number: 27/72.

Transposition: 2 – 2 – 1 – 2 – 1 – 3 – 1.

Features: Sarasangi uses a diatonic lower and chromatic upper tetrachord. It resembles the harmonic major mode of Western music or maqam Shawq Afza of Arabic modal music.

Mela Harikambhoji

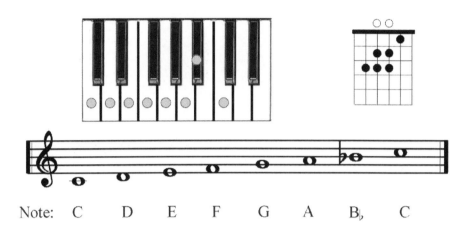

| Note: | C | D | E | F | G | A | B♭ | C |

Origin: Carnatic.

Scale Type: Heptatonic.

Tuning: Just.

Chakra: Bana.

Number: 28/72.

Transposition: 2 – 2 – 1 – 2 – 2 – 1 – 2.

Features: Harikambhoji is a type of diatonic mode, the nearest equivalents to which are the modern Western Mixolydian mode, Khamaj thãt of Northern Hindustani music and Adonai Malach of Klezmer.

Mela Dheerasankarabharanam

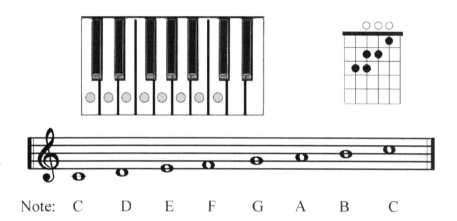

Note: C   D   E   F   G   A   B   C

Origin: Carnatic.

Scale Type: Heptatonic.

Tuning: Just.

Chakra: Bana.

Number: 29/72.

Transposition: 2 – 2 – 1 – 2 – 2 – 2 – 1.

Features: Dheerasankarabharanam is a type of diatonic mode the nearest equivalents to which are the ancient Greek Lydian mode, the modern Western Ionian mode or major scale, Bilawal thāt of Northern Hindustani music and Maqam Ajam of Arabic modal music.

Mela Naganandini

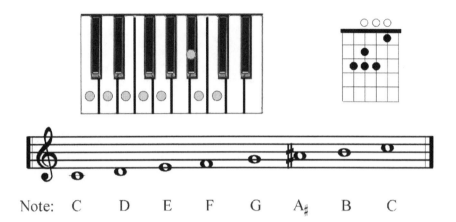

Note: C   D   E   F   G   A♯   B   C

Origin: Carnatic.

Scale Type: Heptatonic.

Tuning: Just.

Chakra: Bana.

Number: 30/72.

Transposition: 2 – 2 – 1 – 2 – 3 – 1 – 1.

Features: Naganandini uses a diatonic lower tetrachord and a chromatic upper tetrachord. A Western musician might think of this mode as a major scale the sixth of which has been raised. Naganandini is one of the modes unique to the mela system.

Mela Yagapriya

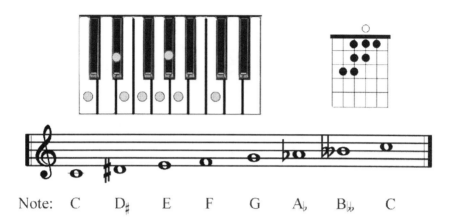

Note: C   D♯   E   F   G   A♭   B♭♭   C

Origin: Carnatic.

Scale Type: Heptatonic.

Tuning: Just.

Chakra: Rutu.

Number: 31/72.

Transposition: 3 – 1 – 1 – 2 – 1 – 1 – 3.

Features: Yagapriya is the first mela belonging to the Rutu chakra. The six mela of the Rutu chakra all have a lower chromatic tetrachord of the type augmented tone, semitone, semitone. Yagapriya is a chromatic mode, using both a lower and an upper chromatic tetrachord. It is one of those modes unique to the mela system.

Mela Ragavardhini

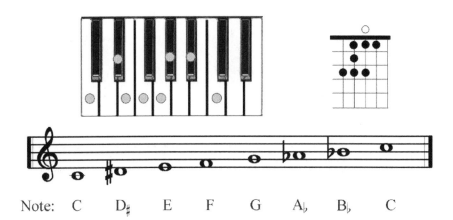

Note: C   D♯   E   F   G   A♭   B♭   C

Origin: Carnatic.

Scale Type: Heptatonic.

Tuning: Just.

Chakra: Rutu.

Number: 32/72.

Transposition: 3 – 1 – 1 – 2 – 1 – 2 – 2.

Features: Ragavardhini uses a chromatic lower and diatonic upper tetrachord to produce a mixed mode. In Greek folk music a similar mode is used which is called Segiah.

Mela Gangeyabhushani

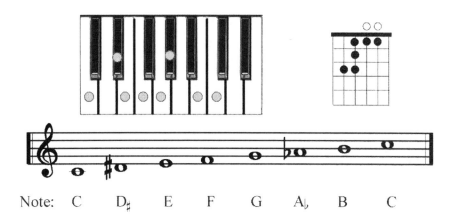

Note: C   D♯   E   F   G   A♭   B   C

Origin: Carnatic.

Scale Type: Heptatonic.

Tuning: Just.

Chakra: Rutu.

Number: 33/72.

Transposition: 3 – 1 – 1 – 2 – 1 – 3 – 1.

Features: Gangeyabhushani is a chromatic mode, using both lower and upper chromatic tetrachords. A similar mode is also used in Greek folk music called Houzam.

Mela Vagadheeswari

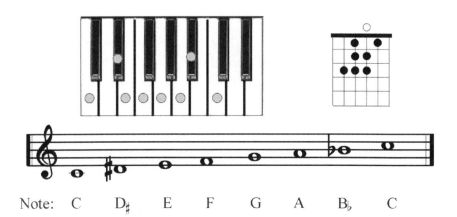

Note: C   D♯   E   F   G   A   B♭   C

Origin: Carnatic.

Scale Type: Heptatonic.

Tuning: Just.

Chakra: Rutu.

Number: 34/72.

Transposition: 3 – 1 – 1 – 2 – 2 – 1 – 2.

Features: Vagadheeswari uses a chromatic lower and diatonic upper tetrachord. It is therefore a mixed mode, the nearest equivalent to which, in Western music is the Mixolydian mode with raised second.

Mela Shulini

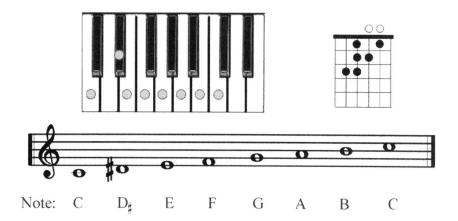

Note: C   D♯   E   F   G   A   B   C

Origin: Carnatic.

Scale Type: Heptatonic.

Tuning: Just.

Chakra: Rutu.

Number: 35/72.

Transposition: 3 – 1 – 1 – 2 – 2 – 2 – 1.

Features: Shulini is also a mixed mode, using a chromatic lower and diatonic upper tetrachord. Shulini is one of the modes which is unique to the mela system.

Mela Chalanata

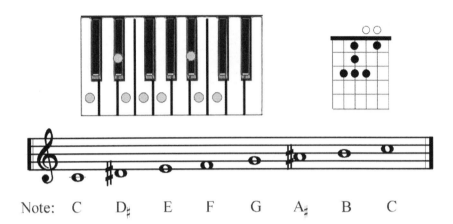

Note: C D♯ E F G A♯ B C

Origin: Carnatic.

Scale Type: Heptatonic.

Tuning: Just.

Chakra: Rutu.

Number: 36/72.

Transposition: 3 – 1 – 1 – 2 – 3 – 1 – 1.

Features: Using both lower and upper chromatic tetrachord, Chalanata is a type of chromatic mode. It is the last of the thirty-six mela belonging to the Madhyama Shuddha group. Chalanata is one of those modes unique to the mela system.

Mela Salagam

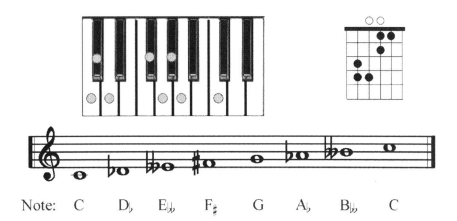

Note: C   D♭   E♭♭   F♯   G   A♭   B♭♭   C

Origin: Carnatic.

Scale Type: Heptatonic.

Tuning: Just.

Chakra: Rishi.

Number: 37/72.

Transposition: 1 – 1 – 4 – 1 – 1 – 1 – 3.

Features: Salagam is not only the first mela of the Rishi chakra, but the first of the thirty-six mela belonging to the Prati Madhyama group, that is mela which use a sharp fourth. Due to this sharp fourth, many of the mela belonging to this group are unique to Carnatic music. Look at the lower tetrachord for example. This consists of two semitones followed by a major third (or more correctly double-augmented second) followed by a semitone. There are no modes in Western music whose lower tetrachord even remotely resembles this.

Mela Jalarnavam

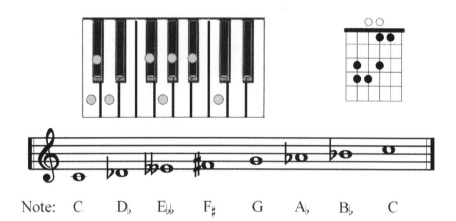

Note: C   D♭   E♭♭   F♯   G   A♭   B♭   C

Origin: Carnatic.

Scale Type: Heptatonic.

Tuning: Just.

Chakra: Rishi.

Number: 38/72.

Transposition: 1 – 1 – 4 – 1 – 1 – 2 – 2.

Features: Due to its characteristic lower tetrachord, mela Jalarnavam is unique to Carnatic music. The upper tetrachord is a familiar form of diatonic tetrachord as found in the natural minor mode for example.

Mela Jhalavarali

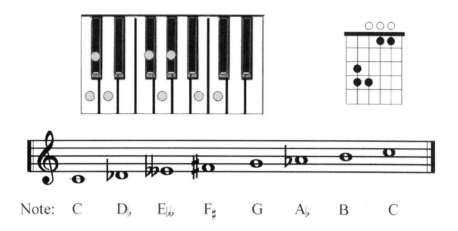

Note: C   D♭   E♭♭   F♯   G   A♭   B   C

Origin: Carnatic.

Scale Type: Heptatonic.

Tuning: Just.

Chakra: Rishi.

Number: 39/72.

Transposition: 1 – 1 – 4 – 1 – 1 – 3 – 1.

Features: Due to its characteristic lower tetrachord, mela Jhalavarali is also unique to Carnatic music. The upper tetrachord is a chromatic tetrachord of the type found in the Western harmonic minor mode.

265

Mela Navaneetam

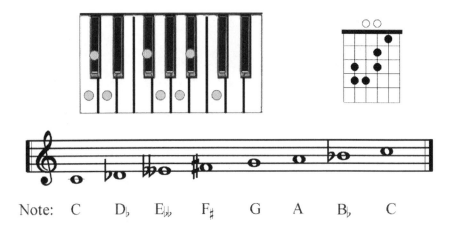

Note: C   D♭   E♭♭   F♯   G   A   B♭   C

Origin: Carnatic.

Scale Type: Heptatonic.

Tuning: Just.

Chakra: Rishi.

Number: 40/72.

Transposition: 1 – 1 – 4 – 1 – 2 – 1 – 2.

Features: Due to its characteristic lower tetrachord, Mela Navaneetam is unique to Carnatic music. The upper tetrachord is a diatonic tetrachord of the type found in say, the Western Dorian mode.

Mela Pavani

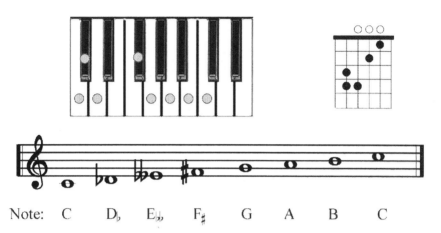

Note: C   D♭   E♭♭   F♯   G   A   B   C

Origin: Carnatic.

Scale Type: Heptatonic.

Tuning: Just.

Chakra: Rishi.

Number: 41/72.

Transposition: 1 – 1 – 4 – 1 – 2 – 2 – 1.

Features: Due to its characteristic lower tetrachord, mela Pavani is unique to Carnatic music. The upper tetrachord is a diatonic tetrachord of the type found in say, the Western major mode.

Mela Raghupriya

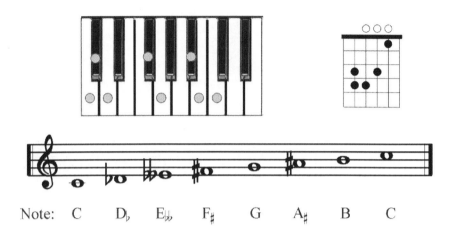

Note: C   D♭   E♭♭   F♯   G   A♯   B   C

Origin: Carnatic.

Scale Type: Heptatonic.

Tuning: Just.

Chakra: Rishi.

Number: 42/72.

Transposition: 1 – 1 – 4 – 1 – 3 – 1 – 1.

Features: Due to its characteristic lower tetrachord, mela Raghupriya is unique to Carnatic music. The upper tetrachord is also a chromatic tetrachord of a type that is rarely found in Western music. This makes mela Raghupriya absolutely unique to the Carnatic system.

Mela Gavambhodi

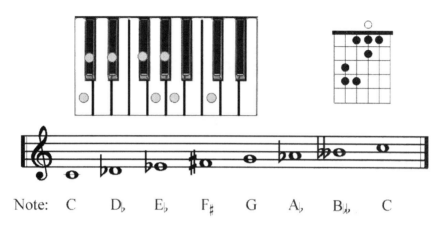

Note: C   D♭   E♭   F♯   G   A♭   B♭♭   C

Origin: Carnatic.

Scale Type: Heptatonic.

Tuning: Just.

Chakra: Vasu.

Number: 43/72.

Transposition: 1 – 2 – 3 – 1 – 1 – 1 – 3.

Features: Gavambhodi is the first mela belonging to the Vasu chakra. The six mela belonging to this chakra all have the same type of lower tetrachord. This consists of a semitone, tone, augmented second and semitone. This type of tetrachord is not generally used in Western music, and can be regarded as being one of those unique contributions that Carnatic music makes to the body of world musical scales in general. .

Mela Bhavapriya

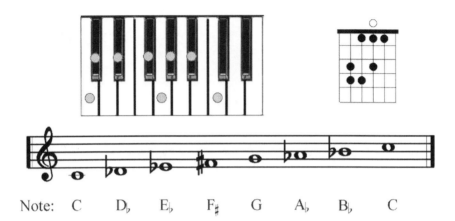

Note: C   D♭   E♭   F♯   G   A♭   B♭   C

Origin: Carnatic.

Scale Type: Heptatonic.

Tuning: Just.

Chakra: Vasu.

Number: 44/72.

Transposition: 1 – 2 – 3 – 1 – 1 – 2 – 2.

Features: Due to its characteristic lower tetrachord, Mela Bhavapriya is unique to Carnatic music. The upper tetrachord is a diatonic tetrachord of the type found in the Western natural minor mode.

Mela Shubhapantuvarali

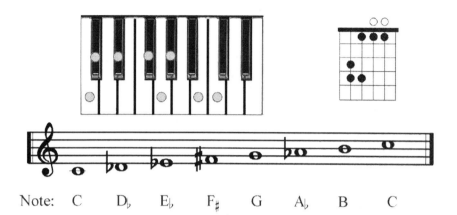

Note: C   D♭   E♭   F♯   G   A♭   B   C

Origin: Carnatic.

Scale Type: Heptatonic.

Tuning: Just.

Chakra: Vasu.

Number: 45/72.

Transposition: 1 – 2 – 3 – 1 – 1 – 3 – 1.

Features: Shubhapantuvarali has an equivalent in the Todi Thāt of Northern Hindustani music. It is also similar to maqam Athar Kurd of Arabic modal music.

Mela Shadvidamargini

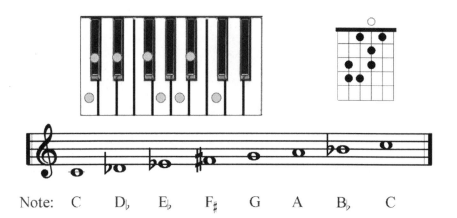

Note: C   D♭   E♭   F♯   G   A   B♭   C

Origin: Carnatic.

Scale Type: Heptatonic.

Tuning: Just.

Chakra: Vasu.

Number: 46/72.

Transposition: 1 – 2 – 3 – 1 – 2 – 1 – 2.

Features: Due to its characteristic lower tetrachord, mela Shadvidamargini is unique to Carnatic music. The upper tetrachord is a diatonic tetrachord of a type found in say, the Western Dorian mode.

Mela Suvarnangi

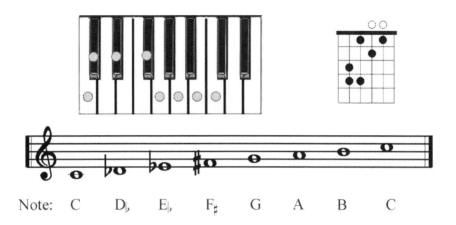

Note: C   D♭   E♭   F♯   G   A   B   C

Origin: Carnatic.

Scale Type: Heptatonic.

Tuning: Just.

Chakra: Vasu.

Number: 47/72.

Transposition: 1 – 2 – 3 – 1 – 2 – 2 – 1.

Features: Due to its characteristic lower tetrachord, mela Suvarnangi is unique to Carnatic music. The upper tetrachord is a diatonic tetrachord of a type found in say, the Western major mode.

Mela Divyamani

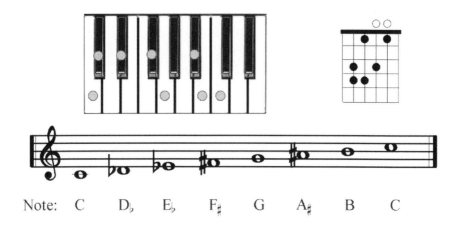

Note: C   D♭   E♭   F♯   G   A♯   B   C

Origin: Carnatic.

Scale Type: Heptatonic.

Tuning: Just.

Chakra: Vasu.

Number: 48/72.

Transposition: 1 – 2 – 3 – 1 – 3 – 1 – 1.

Features: Due to both the characteristic lower and upper tetrachord, mela Divyamani is unique to Carnatic music.

Mela Dhavalambari

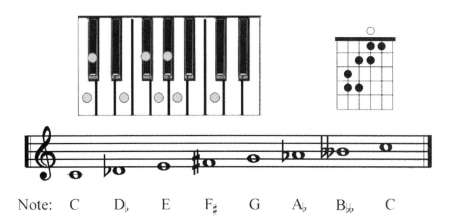

Note: C   D♭   E   F♯   G   A♭   B♭♭   C

Origin: Carnatic.

Scale Type: Heptatonic.

Tuning: Just.

Chakra: Brahma.

Number: 49/72.

Transposition: 1 – 3 – 2 – 1 – 1 – 1 – 3.

Features: Dhavalambari is the first mela belonging to the Brahma chakra. All six mela in this group are notable for their characteristic lower tetrachord consisting of semitone, augmented second, tone and semitone. This tetrachord is not generally used in Western music. The upper tetrachord is a chromatic tetrachord of a type which is also not generally used in the West. This gives mela Dhavalambari a very unique profile.

Mela Namanarayani

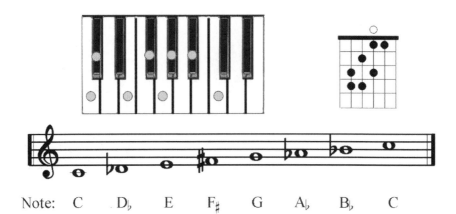

Note: C   D♭   E   F♯   G   A♭   B♭   C

Origin: Carnatic.

Scale Type: Heptatonic.

Tuning: Just.

Chakra: Brahma.

Number: 50/72.

Transposition: 1 – 3 – 2 – 1 – 1 – 2 – 2.

Features: Due to its characteristic lower tetrachord, mela Namanarayani is unique to Carnatic music. A Western musician might think of this mode as a minor Lydian mode the second of which has been flattened.

Mela Kamavardani

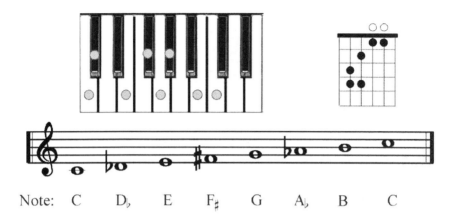

Note: C   D♭   E   F♯   G   A♭   B   C

Origin: Carnatic.

Scale Type: Heptatonic.

Tuning: Just.

Chakra: Brahma.

Number: 51/72.

Transposition: 1 – 3 – 2 – 1 – 1 – 3 – 1.

Features: Kamavardini has a correspondence with Northern Hindustani music in the form of Purvi Thāt.

Mela Ramapriya

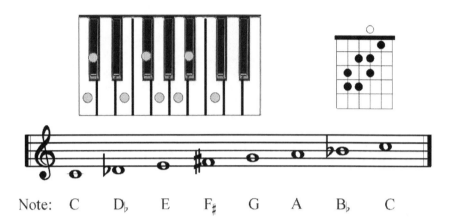

Note: C   D♭   E   F♯   G   A   B♭   C

Origin: Carnatic.

Scale Type: Heptatonic.

Tuning: Just.

Chakra: Brahma.

Number: 52/72.

Transposition: 1 – 3 – 2 – 1 – 2 – 1 – 2.

Features: Due to its characteristic lower tetrachord, mela Ramapriya is unique to Carnatic music. A Western musician might think of this mode as an acoustic scale the second of which has been flattened.

Mela Gamanashrama

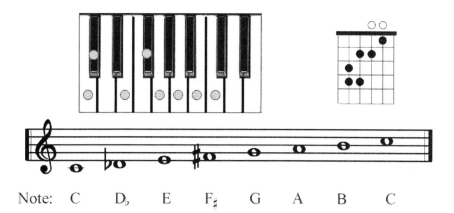

| Note: | C | D♭ | E | F♯ | G | A | B | C |

Origin: Carnatic.

Scale Type: Heptatonic.

Tuning: Just.

Chakra: Brahma.

Number: 53/72.

Transposition: 1 – 3 – 2 – 1 – 2 – 2 – 1.

Features: Gamanashrama has an equivalent in Marwa Thãt of Northern Hindustani music. A Western musician might think of this mode as a Lydian mode the second of which has been flattened – a Neapolitan form of Lydian mode in other words.

Mela Vishwambari

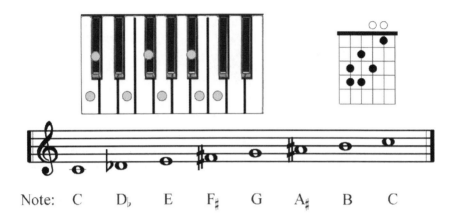

Note: C   D♭   E   F♯   G   A♯   B   C

Origin: Carnatic.

Scale Type: Heptatonic.

Tuning: Just.

Chakra: Brahma.

Number: 54/72.

Transposition: 1 – 3 – 2 – 1 – 3 – 1 – 1.

Features: Neither the lower or upper tetrachords of mela Vishwambari are generally used in Western music. This makes mela Vishwambari unique to Carnatic music.

Mela Shamalangi

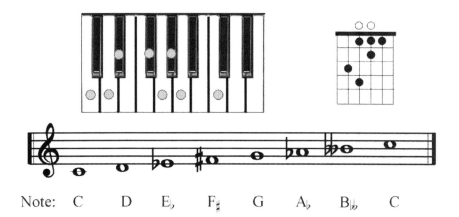

Note: C   D   E♭   F♯   G   A♭   B♭♭   C

Origin: Carnatic.

Scale Type: Heptatonic.

Tuning: Just.

Chakra: Disi.

Number: 55/72.

Transposition: 2 – 1 – 3 – 1 – 1 – 1 – 3.

Features: Shamalangi is the first mela belonging to the Disi chakra. The six mela belonging to this group all use a lower tetrachord of a type which is familiar to Western musicians, being found in modes such as the Hungarian minor. The upper tetrachord however, is a chromatic tetrachord not generally used in the West. This makes mela Shamalangi unique to Carnatic music.

Mela Shanmukhapriya

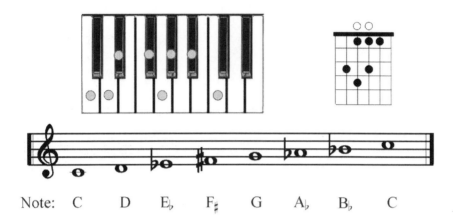

Note: C   D   E♭   F♯   G   A♭   B♭   C

Origin: Carnatic.

Scale Type: Heptatonic.

Tuning: Just.

Chakra: Disi.

Number: 56/72.

Transposition: 2 – 1 – 3 – 1 – 1 – 2 – 2.

Features: Shanmukhapriya has an equivalent in Western music where it appears as one of the forms of the Hungarian minor mode.

Mela Simhendramadhyamam

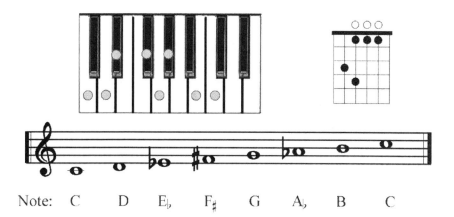

Note:	C	D	E♭	F♯	G	A♭	B	C

Origin: Carnatic.

Scale Type: Heptatonic.

Tuning: Just.

Chakra: Disi.

Number: 57/72.

Transposition: 2 – 1 – 3 – 1 – 1 – 3 – 1.

Features: Simhendramadhyamam has an equivalent in Western music where it appears as one of the forms of the Hungarian minor mode. It also has a correspondence in Niaventi, one of the modes of Greek folk music.

Mela Hemavati

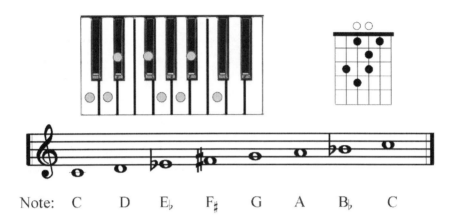

Note: C   D   E♭   F♯   G   A   B♭   C

Origin: Carnatic.

Scale Type: Heptatonic.

Tuning: Just.

Chakra: Disi.

Number: 58/72.

Transposition: 2 – 1 – 3 – 1 – 2 – 1 – 2.

Features: Hamavati has an equivalent in Western music where it is known as the Ukrainian Dorian, Doina in Klezmer; Souzenak in Greek folk music and maqam Nakriz in Arabic modal music.

Mela Dharmavati

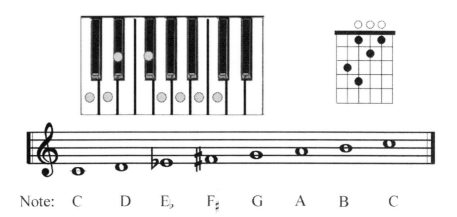

Note: C   D   E♭   F♯   G   A   B   C

Origin: Carnatic.

Scale Type: Heptatonic.

Tuning: Just.

Chakra: Disi.

Number: 59/72.

Transposition: 2 – 1 – 3 – 1 – 2 – 2 – 1.

Features: Dharavati has an equivalent in Western music in the form of the Lydian diminished mode – a Lydian mode with flat third.

Mela Neetimati

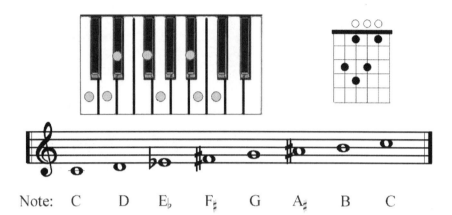

Note: C   D   E♭   F♯   G   A♯   B   C

Origin: Carnatic.

Scale Type: Heptatonic.

Tuning: Just.

Chakra: Disi.

Number: 60/72.

Transposition: 2 – 1 – 3 – 1 – 3 – 1 – 1.

Features: Due to its characteristic upper chromatic tetrachord, a type not generally used in Western music, mela Neetimati is unique to Carnatic music.

Mela Kantamani

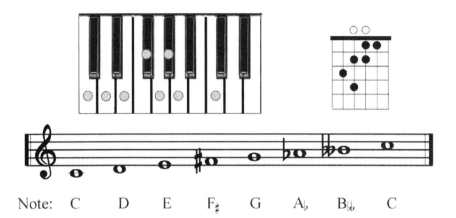

Note: C   D   E   F♯   G   A♭   B♭♭   C

Origin: Carnatic.

Scale Type: Heptatonic.

Tuning: Just.

Chakra: Rudra.

Number: 61/72.

Transposition: 2 – 2 – 2 – 1 – 1 – 1 – 3.

Features: Kantamani is the first mela belonging to the Rudra chakra. The six mela in this group all use a lower tetrachord familiar to Western musicians as the lower tetrachord of the Lydiaan mode. The type of chromatic tetrachord used by mela Kanatamani however, makes this mode unique to Carnatic music.

Mela Rishabhapriya

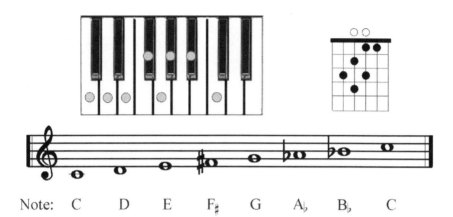

Note: C   D   E   F♯   G   A♭   B♭   C

Origin: Carnatic.

Scale Type: Heptatonic.

Tuning: Just.

Chakra: Rudra.

Number: 62/72.

Transposition: 2 – 2 – 2 – 1 – 1 – 2 – 2.

Features: Mela Rishabhapriya has a direct equivalent in Western music where it is known as the Lydian minor mode.

Mela Latangi

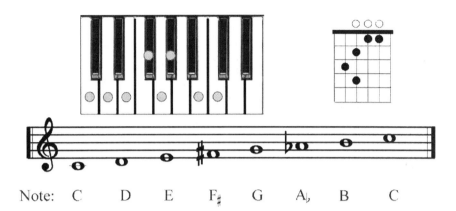

Note: C   D   E   F♯   G   A♭   B   C

Origin: Carnatic.

Scale Type: Heptatonic.

Tuning: Just.

Chakra: Rudra.

Number: 63/72.

Transposition: 2 – 2 – 2 – 1 – 1 – 3 – 1.

Features: Mela Latangi has a profile which, to a Western musician would appear as a Lydian mode the sixth of which has been flattened.

Mela Vachaspati

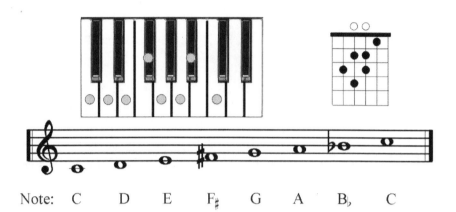

| Note: | C | D | E | F♯ | G | A | B♭ | C |

Origin: Carnatic.

Scale Type: Heptatonic.

Tuning: Just.

Chakra: Rudra.

Number: 64/72.

Transposition: 2 – 2 – 2 – 1 – 2 – 1 – 2.

Features: Vachaspati has an equivalent in Western music in the form of the acoustic scale, otherwise known as the harmonic Lydian

Mela Mechakalyani

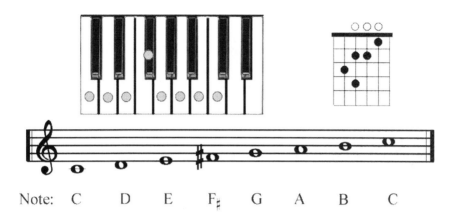

Note: C   D   E   F♯   G   A   B   C

Origin: Carnatic.

Scale Type: Heptatonic.

Tuning: Just.

Chakra: Rudra.

Number: 65/72.

Transposition: 2 – 2 – 2 – 1 – 2 – 2 – 1.

Features: Mechakalyani is a diatonic mode, recognized in Northern Hindustani music as Kalyan Thāt. In Western music Mechakalyani is equivalent to the Lydian mode.

Mela Chitrambari

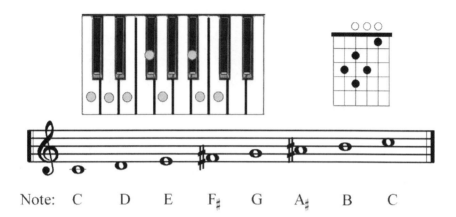

Note: C   D   E   F♯   G   A♯   B   C

Origin: Carnatic.

Scale Type: Heptatonic.

Tuning: Just.

Chakra: Rudra.

Number: 66/72.

Transposition: 2 – 2 – 2 – 1 – 3 – 1 – 1.

Features: Although using a familiar Lydian type lower tetrachord, mela Chitrambari uses a chromatic upper tetrachord of a type rarely used in Western music. This makes mela Chitrambari unique to the Carnatic system.

Mela Sucharitra

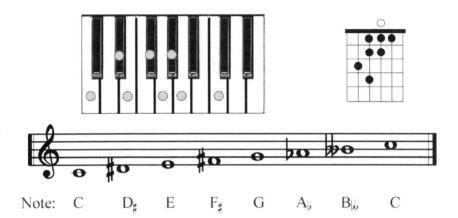

Note: C   D♯   E   F♯   G   A♭   B♭♭   C

Origin: Carnatic.

Scale Type: Heptatonic.

Tuning: Just.

Chakra: Aditya.

Number: 67/72.

Transposition: 3 – 1 – 2 – 1 – 1 – 1 – 3.

Features: Unique to Carnatic music, Sucharitra is the first mela belonging to the Aditya chakra. Mela belonging to this group all have a Lydian type lower tetrachord except for a vital difference – the second is characteristically raised. This produces a tetrachord of a type familiar to Western musicians through modes such as the Hungarian major or the Greek folk mode Periaiotikos. .

Mela Jyoti Swarupini

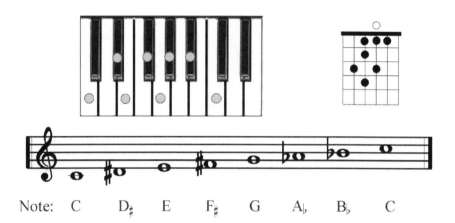

| Note: | C | D♯ | E | F♯ | G | A♭ | B♭ | C |

Origin: Carnatic.

Scale Type: Heptatonic.

Tuning: Just.

Chakra: Aditya.

Number: 68/72.

Transposition: 3 – 1 – 2 – 1 – 1 – 2 – 2.

Features: Mela Jyoti Swarupini has a profile which is similar to the Hungarian major mode, the only difference being the flat sixth. This makes Mela Jyoti Swarupini unique to Carnatic music.

Mela Dhatuvardani

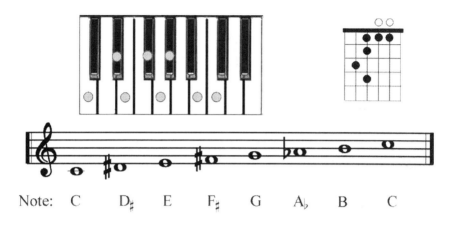

Note: C D♯ E F♯ G A♭ B C

Origin: Carnatic.

Scale Type: Heptatonic.

Tuning: Just.

Chakra: Aditya.

Number: 69/72.

Transposition: 3 – 1 – 2 – 1 – 1 – 3 – 1.

Features: Mela Dhatuvardani combines a lower tetrachord, familiar to Western musicians as that used in the Hungarian major mode, with a chromatic upper tetrachord, also familiar in the West as the type found in the harmonic minor mode. This gives rise to a mode which is unique to Carnatic music.

Mela Nasikabhushani

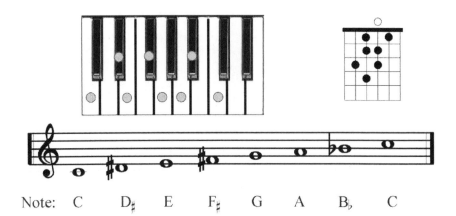

Note: C D♯ E F♯ G A B♭ C

Origin: Carnatic.

Scale Type: Heptatonic.

Tuning: Just.

Chakra: Aditya.

Number: 70/72.

Transposition: 3 – 1 – 2 – 1 – 2 – 1 – 2.

Features: Nasikabhushani has an equivalent in Western music as one of the forms of the Hungarian major mode.

Mela Kosalam

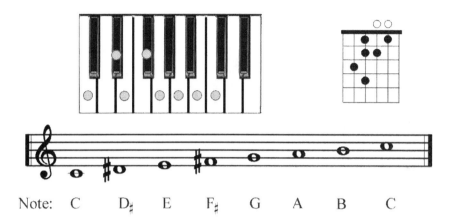

Note: C   D♯   E   F♯   G   A   B   C

Origin: Carnatic.

Scale Type: Heptatonic.

Tuning: Just.

Chakra: Aditya.

Number: 71/72.

Transposition: 3 – 1 – 2 – 1 – 2 – 2 – 1.

Features: Kosalam also has an equivalent in Western music, where it appears as another form of the Hungarian major mode. In Greek folk music a similar mode is used which is called Peraiotikos.

Mela Rasikapriya

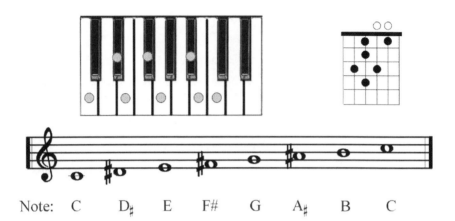

Note: C   D♯   E   F#   G   A♯   B   C

Origin: Carnatic.

Scale Type: Heptatonic.

Tuning: Just.

Chakra: Aditya.

Number: 72/72.

Transposition: 3 – 1 – 2 – 1 – 3 – 1 – 1.

Features: With mela Rasikapriya we reach the last of the seventy-two modes belonging to the Carnatic mela system. A Western musician might think of this mode as a Lydian mode the second and sixth of which have been sharpened. This gives rise to a mode not generally used in the West, making at again, unique to Carnatic music.

Section 14: Inventing Your Own Scales

If there is a lesson to be learned from the great range of scales presented in this book, it is probably that there is no need to limit our musical explorations to a few well-known and probably over-used scales. Indeed, aside from those presented here there is great potential for invention as far as musical scales are concerned.

This process of invention can and has been occurring among musicians in every imaginable direction. In the last century alone productive experiments have been made along lines such as:

- scales whose pattern exceeds the octave;

- scales having very few notes;

- scales that divide the octave equally, although using a different number than twelve;

- scales that are tuned after the fashion of ancient Greek or Mesopotamian lyre tunings;

- scales based on the intervals of the harmonic series, in particular the prime numbered harmonics beyond the Western limit of five;

- scales based on smaller intervals than a semitone i.e. quarter tone or one-third tone scales;

- scales based on non-harmonic proportions such as the Golden Mean;

- etc., etc.

In simple terms, the sky is the limit and even though such experiments often yield sounds which are unfamiliar to the listener and therefore lack any popular or commercial potential, it is entirely possible that some time soon, experimentation in this area may yield an altogether new sound which is so alluring and appealing to the listener that it goes on to provide the stimulus for a complete revolution in the language of music so far as the West conceives it.

Recommended Reading

Abate, E. (2009). Ethiopian Kinit. *Proceedings of the 16th International Conference of Ethiopian Studies*. Trondheim: http://portal.svt.ntnu.no/sites/ices16/Proceedings/Volume%204/Ezra%20Abate%20-%20Ethiopian%20Ki%C3%B1it.pdf.

Baker, D. (1988). *How to Play Bebop (Vols. I, II & III)*. Van Nuys: Alfred Publishing Company.

Barbour, J. M. (March, 1929). Synthetic Musical Scales. *The American Mathematical Monthly, Vol. 36, No. 3*, 155 - 160.

Belaiev, V. (1963). The Formation of Folk Modal Systems. *Journal of the International Folk Music Council, Vol. 15*, 4 - 9.

Busoni, F. (2012). *Sketch of a New Esthetic of Music*, Forgotten Books. Charleston.

Clarke, H. L. (Vol. 18, No. 4, June, 1960). Musical Scales Ad Hoc and Ad Hominem. *The Journal of Aesthetics and Art Criticism*, 472 - 474.

Cormier, S. (2006). *Modal Music Composition: Expanded Edition*. Arlington: Inman & Artz Publishers.

Danielou, A. (1979). *Introduction to the Study of Musical Scales*. Columbia: South Asia Books.

Danielou, A. (1995). *Music and the Power of Sound: the Influence of Tuning and Interval on Consciousness*. Inner Traditions: Vermont.

Danielou, A. (1968). *Northern Indian Music*. New York: Frederick A. Praeger.

Danielou, A. (1968). *The Ragas of Northern Indian Music*. London: Barrie

& Jenkins.

Day-O'Connel, J. (2007). *Pentatonicism from the Eighteenth Century to Debussy*. Rochester: University of Rochester Press.

Ellis, A. (1885). On the Musical Scales of Various Nations. *Journal of the Society of Arts, No. 33* .

Garfias, R. (1976). *Music of a Thousand Autumns: the Tōgaku Style of Japanese Court Music*. Los Angeles: University of California Press.

Garfias, R. (1975). Preliminary Thoughts on Burmese Modes. *Asian Music, Vol. 7, No. 1* , 39 - 49.

Garfias, R. (n.d.). The Sacred Mi-Kagura of the Japanese Imperial Court. *Selected Reports, Vol. 1, Issues 2 - 3, University of California (Los Angeles), Institute of Ethnomusicology* , 150 - 181.

Helmholtz, H. (1954). *On the Sensations of Tone*. New York: Dover Publications.

Hewitt, M (2001). *The Tonal Phoenix*. Orpheus-Verlag, Bonn.

Hewitt, M (2008). *Musical Theory for Computer Musicians*. Cengage, Boston.

Hewitt, M (2010). *Composition for Computer Musicians*. Cengage, Boston.

Hewitt, M (2011). *Harmony for Computer Musicians*. Cengage, Boston.

King, A (1972). The Construction and Tuning of the Kora. *African Language Studies 13*; 113 – 136.

Krilov, K. S. (2007). *Harmony in Bulgarian Music* . PhD Thesis: University of Oregon.

Kunst, J. (1949). *Music in Java*. The Hague: M. Nijhoff.

Lindsay, J. (1992). *Javanese Gamelan: Traditional Orchestras of Indonesia*. New York: Oxford University Press.

Lu-Ting, H., & Kuo'-huang, H. (1982). On Chinese Scales and National Modes. *Asian Music, Vol. 14, No. 1*, 132 - 154.

McPhee, C. (2000). *A House in Bali*. Rutland: Tuttle Publishing.

McPhee, C. (1966). *Music in Bali: A Study in Form and Instrumental Organization in Balinese Orchestral Music*. Yale: Yale University Press.

Mellers, W. (1981). God, Modality and Meaning in Some Recent Songs of Bob Dylan. *Popular Music*, 142 - 157.

Morton, D. (1976). *The Traditional Music of Thailand*. University of California Press.

Oke, V. *22 Shrutis*. Retrieved from: http://www.22shruti.com.

Orenstein, A. (1991). *Ravel: Man and Music*. New York: Dover Publications.

Partch, H. (1974). *Genesis of a Music*. New York: Da Capo Press.

Pike, L. (April, 2001). Tonality and Modality in Sibelius's Sixth Symphony . *Tempo, New Series, No. 216.*, 6-16.

Ridenour, W. (2010). *The Kora and Korafolaw: A Treatise on the Musical Instrument and Those Who Play It*. Retrieved from ISP Collection. Paper 833: http://digitalcollections.sit.edu/isp_collection/833

Sachs, C. (1962). *The Wellsprings of Music*. The Hague: Martinus Nijhoff.

Sharp, C. (1907). *English Folk Song: Some Conclusions*. London: Novello.

Sharp, C. (2010). *English Folk Songs from the Southern Appalachians*. Whitefish: Kessinger.

Sharp, C. (1908). Some Characteristics of English Folk Song. *Folklore Vol. 19, No. 2, Jan.*, 132 - 152.

Sharp, C., & Broadwood, L. E. (June 30, 1908). Some Characteristics of English Folk Music. *Folklore Vol.. 19, No. 2*, 132 - 152.

Sharp, C., & Manson, C. L. (1909). *Folk Songs from Somerset*. London.

Slominsky, N. (Jan. 1947). Roy Harris. *The Music Quarterly, Vol. 33, No. 1*, 17 - 37.

Slonimsky, N. (1999). *Thesaurus of Scales and Melodic Patterns*. New York: Schirmer Books.

Smith, R. L. (1977). *Debussy on Music*. New York: Alfred A. Knopf.

Tallmadge, W. (Autumn, 1984). Blue Notes and Blue Tonality. *The Black Perspective in Music, Vol. 12, No. 2* , 155 - 165.

Tcherepnin, A. (2010). *Basic Elements of My Musical Language*. Retrieved August 2011, from The Tcherepnin Society: http://www.tcherepnin.com/alex/basic_elem1.htm

Tenzier, M. (2000). *Gamelan Gong Kebyar: the Art of Twentieth Century Balinese Music*. Chicago: University of Chicago Press.

Vargyas, L. (1958). Some Parallels of Modal Structures in Western and Eastern Europe. *Journal of the International Folk Music Council, Vol. 10* , 22 - 28.

Vitale, W. (2002). Balinese Kebyar Music Breaks the Five Tone Barrier: New Composition for Seven-Tone Gamelan. *Perspectives of New Music, Vol. 40, No. 1* , 5 - 69.

Zabolcsi, B. (Jan. - Dec. 1943). Five-Tone Scales and Civilization. *Acta Musicologica, Vol. 15, Fasc. 1/4* , 24 - 34.

Zganec, V. (1958). The Tonal and Modal Structure of Yugoslav Folk Music. *Journal of the Internatinal Folk Music Council, Vol. 10.* , 18 - 21.

About the Author

Dr Mike Hewitt is a composer, author and lecturer currently living in North Wales. He earned a bachelor of music degree from the University of London and a master of music degree and doctorate from the University of North Wales, Bangor. He is author of numerous books on music, including the popular series of books for computer musicians. These include *Music Theory for Computer Musicians; Composition for Computer Musicians* and *Harmony for Computer Musicians.*